NEW BRIGHTON HIGH SCHOOL
NEW BRIGHTON, PA 15066

THE HOLOCAUST LIBRARY

Nazi War Criminals

by

EARLE RICE JR.

NEW BRIGHTON HIGH SCHOOL
NEW BRIGHTON. PA 15066

Lucent Books, P.O. Box 289011, San Diego, CA 92198-9011

Books in the Holocaust Library

No part of this book may be reproduced or used in any other form or by any other means, electrical, mechanical, or otherwise, including, but not limited to, photocopy, recording, or any information storage and retrieval system, without prior written permission from the publisher.

Library of Congress Cataloging-in-Publication Data

Rice, Earle
  Nazi war criminals / by Earle Rice, Jr.
    p. cm. —
  "The Holocaust library."
  Includes bibliographical references and index.
  Summary: Explores the lives of six Nazi war criminals and the roles they played in implementing the Final Solution to the Jewish Question.
  ISBN 1-56006-097-2 (alk. paper)
  1. Nuremberg Trial of Major German War Criminals, Nuremberg, Germany, 1945–1946—Juvenile literature. 2. War crime trials—Germany—Nuremberg—Juvenile literature. [1. Nuremberg Trial of Major German War Criminals, Nuremberg, Germany, 1945–1946. 2. War crime trials.]
  I. Title.
JX5437.8.R52 1998
341.6'90268—dc21
                                                     97-9811
                                                       CIP
                                                        AC

Copyright 1998 by Lucent Books, Inc., P.O. Box 289011,
San Diego, CA 92198-9011

Table of Contents

Foreword

More than eleven million innocent people, mostly Jews but also millions of others deemed "subhuman" by Adolf Hitler such as Gypsies, Russians, and Poles, were murdered by the Germans during World War II. The magnitude and unique horror of the Holocaust continues to make it a focal point in history—not only the history of modern times, but also the entire record of humankind. While the war itself temporarily changed the political landscape, the Holocaust forever changed the way we look at ourselves.

Starting with the European Renaissance in the 1400s, continuing through the Enlightenment of the 1700s, and extending to the Liberalism of the 1800s, philosophers and others developed the idea that people's intellect and reason allowed them to rise above their animal natures and conquer poverty, brutality, warfare, and all manner of evils. Given the will to do so, there was no height to which humanity might not rise. Was not mankind, these people argued, the noblest creation of God—in the words of the Bible, "a little lower than the angels"?

Western Europeans believed so heartily in these concepts that when rumors of mass murders by the Nazis began to emerge, people refused to accept—despite mounting evidence—that such things could take place. Even the Jews who were being deported to the death camps had a hard time believing that they were headed toward extermination. Rational beings, they argued, could not commit such actions. When the veil of secrecy was finally ripped from the death camps, however, the world recoiled in shock and horror. If humanity was capable of such depravity, what was its true nature? Were humans lower even than animals instead of just beneath the angels?

The perpetration of the Holocaust, so far outside the bounds of society's experience, cried out for explanations. For more than a half century, people have sought them. Thousands of books, diaries, sermons, poems, plays, films, and lectures have been devoted to almost every imaginable aspect of the Holocaust, yet it remains one of the most difficult episodes in history to understand.

Some scholars have explained the Holocaust as a uniquely German event, pointing to the racial supremacy theories of German philosophers, the rigidity of German society, and the tradition of obedience to authority. Others have seen it as a uniquely Jewish phenomenon, the culmination of centuries of anti-Semitism in Christian Europe. Still others have said that the Holocaust was a unique combination of these two factors—a set of circumstances unlikely ever to recur.

Such explanations are comfortable and simple—too simple. The Holocaust was neither a German event nor a Jewish event. It was a human event. The same forces—racism, prejudice, fanaticism—that sent millions to the gas chambers have not disappeared. If anything, they have become more evident. One cannot say, "It can't happen again." On a different scale, it has happened again. More than a million Cambodians were killed between 1974 and 1979 by a Communist government. In 1994 thousands of innocent civilians were murdered in tribal warfare between the Hutu and Tutsi tribes in the African nations of Burundi and Rwanda. Christian Serbs in Bosnia embarked on a program of "ethnic cleansing" in the mid-1990s, seeking to rid the country of Muslims.

The complete answer to the Holocaust has proved elusive. Indeed, it may never be found. The search, however, must continue. As author Elie Wiesel, a survivor of the death camps, wrote, "No one has the right to speak for the dead. . . . Still, the story had to be told. In spite of all risks, all possible misunderstandings. It needed to be told for the sake of our children."

Each book in Lucent Books' seven volume Holocaust Library covers a different topic that reveals the full gamut of human response to the Holocaust. *The Nazis, The Final Solution, The Death Camps and Nazi War Criminals* focus on the perpetrators of the Holocaust and their plan to eliminate the Jewish people. Volumes on *The Righteous Gentiles, The Resistance,* and *The Survivors* reveal that humans are capable of being "the noblest creation of God—" people can still commit acts of bravery and altruism even in the most terrible circumstances.

History offers a way to interpret and reinterpret the past and an opportunity to alter the future. Lucent Books' topic-centered approach is an ideal introduction for students to study such phenomena as the Holocaust. After all, only by becoming knowledgeable about such atrocities can humanity hope to prevent future crimes from occurring. Although such historical lessons seem clear and unavoidable, as historian Yehuda Bauer wrote, "People seldom learn from history. Can we be an exception?"

Chronology of Events

1923

Julius Streicher founds *Der Stürmer*, an anti-Semitic weekly newspaper.

1925

Streicher named *Gauleiter* (district leader) of Franconia.

1929

January 6 Adolf Hitler appoints Himmler *Reichsführer-SS*.

1932

July Himmler appoints Heydrich chief of SS security (which later evolved into the SD).

1933

January 30 Hitler appointed chancellor of the German government; the Nazis take power; Streicher elected to the Reichstag.

March 22 Himmler establishes the first concentration camp for political prisoners at Dachau.

April 1 Streicher heads boycott against Jewish shops and offices.

1934

April 20 Hitler names Himmler to head the Prussian Police and the Gestapo.

June Höss joins SS and begins assignment at Dachau as a noncommissioned officer.

June 29–30 The Night of the Long Knives; Himmler's SS purges the rival SA in a bloodbath ordered by Hitler; Heydrich plays a key role.

1936

June 17 Hitler appoints Himmler to head the newly unified German police.

1938

August Eichmann named to head the SS Office for Jewish Emigration in Vienna.

August 1 Höss transferred from Dachau to Sachsenhausen concentration camp to serve as camp adjutant.

November 10 Streicher speaks out publicly in support of the pogrom staged by the Nazis on *Kristallnacht*—the Night of Broken Glass.

1939

August Heydrich stages a mock raid on a German radio station near the Polish border to provide Hitler with an excuse to invade Poland.

September 1 Germans invade Poland; World War II begins.

September 27 Warsaw falls to the Germans; Heydrich appointed head of RSHA.

December 25 Höss elevated to camp executive officer at Sachsenhausen.

1940

May 1 Höss promoted to captain and appointed commandant of Auschwitz.

December Eichmann named chief of the Gestapo's Section IV B4, dealing with Jewish affairs and evacuation.

1941

June 22 Germany invades the Soviet Union; plans for the Final Solution start to take shape.

July 31 Reich Marshal Hermann Göring directs Reinhard Heydrich to make preparations for the Final Solution.

September 15 Höss experiments using Cyclon B on Russian prisoners of war at Auschwitz.

September 27 Hitler appoints Heydrich deputy Reich protector for Bohemia and Moravia.

1942

January 20 Heydrich convenes the Wannsee Conference; Eichmann records the minutes of the meeting that formalized plans for the Final Solution.

March Cyclon B system adopted permanently at Auschwitz.

May 27 Free Czech agents attempt to assassinate Heydrich.

June 4 Heydrich dies of wounds received eight days earlier.

1943

May Mengele—after serving on the eastern and western fronts with the Waffen-SS—appointed chief doctor at Auschwitz.

November 22 Command divided at Auschwitz-Birkenau complex; Höss assumes new duties as chief of concentration camp inspectors.

1944

May Extermination process at Auschwitz reaches peak efficiency; more than nine thousand victims reported killed daily.

1945

April 30 Hitler commits suicide.

May 8 Germany surrenders unconditionally to the Allies; World War II in Europe ends.

May 23 Himmler commits suicide.

August 8 London Agreement signed by the Allies, providing for the prosecution of Nazi war criminals.

November 20 Trial of twenty-two major Nazi war criminals commences.

1946

March 11 Höss arrested by the British Field Security Police and turned over to Polish authorities about two weeks later.

October 1 The International Military Tribunal returns verdicts against twenty-two major Nazi war criminals in Nuremberg.

October 16 Ten convicted Nazi war criminals, including Streicher, hanged at Nuremberg.

November Second phase of war crimes trials begins in Nuremberg and lasts until April 1949; third phase of trials continue elsewhere to this day.

1947

March 27 Höss—after being tried and found guilty—sentenced to death by a Polish tribunal.

April 7 Höss hanged at Auschwitz.

1962

May 31 Eichmann hanged in Israel's Ramleh prison for crimes against the Jews and crimes against humanity.

1985

Human remains disinterred at Embu, Brazil, declared to be those of Mengele.

Of Courts, Crimes, and Criminals

Commencing with Adolf Hitler's appointment as chancellor of Germany's Third Reich on January 30, 1933, the Germans embarked on the intentional, systematic destruction of European Jewry. From 1933 through 1939, the Germans first stripped the Jews of their rights as citizens, then encouraged half of Germany's 550,000 Jews to emigrate to other parts of Europe and the world. Those Jews who chose to stay in Germany soon became victims of vicious German persecution.

On September 1, 1939, Hitler—on the premise that Germany's expanding population needed more *Lebensraum* (living space)—invaded Poland, thereby igniting World War II. Shortly thereafter the Germans expelled all Jews from Germany proper and forcibly relocated them to their newly acquired territories in the east. As Hitler's aggression expanded the sphere of German influence—first to Poland in the east, then to Denmark, Norway, Belgium, the Netherlands, Luxembourg, and France in the west—more and more Jews came under German control.

With Germany's invasion of the Soviet Union on June 22, 1941, Hitler began to look critically at the cost of relocating and incarcerating Jews in the Eastern Territories as an impediment to the German war effort. Dr. Louis L. Snyder, an eminent scholar of German history, writes:

The year 1941 marked a turning point in the [Germans'] anti-Jewish campaign. . . . Enmeshed in total war, [Hitler] saw Jews in the

A Jewish family is forced to emigrate from its hometown in Germany in 1939. In the background, uniformed Nazis laugh and jeer at the family's misery.

way of victory. Several million Jews were incarcerated in Polish ghettos. Emigration was costly. A policy initiated in 1940 to expel the Jews to Africa had failed. Hitler decided on a drastic move. At this time the idea of a "final solution," or what he called a "territorial solution," began to form in his mind. The plan called for the complete elimination of European Jewry.[1]

In practice, Hitler's plan resulted in the annihilation of approximately six million Jews by war's end, or about one-third of the world's Jewish population when the war began in 1939.

Evidence of German Bestialities

The Germans referred to their program of organized mass murder as "the Final Solution of the Jewish question" (*die Endlösung der Judenfrage*).[2] Their wholesale slaughter of European Jews is more widely known today as the Holocaust—a Greek word used in the Bible to designate a burnt offering to the gods that is completely consumed by fire. During the Holocaust, the corpses of several million innocent victims of the German scourge were reduced to ashes in open-pit incinerators and in the furnaces of death camp crematoria.

The Germans carried out this huge pogrom—that is, the organized massacre of helpless people—in strict secrecy, managing to conceal and contain their crimes within borders closed by war. Throughout most of the war, only scattered rumors of German atrocities slipped across the tightly controlled boundaries of Nazi-occupied Europe. At first, observers in the outside world greeted such rumors with disbelief and denial. The enormity of the crimes committed by the Germans in their attempt to render Europe

Judenfrei (cleansed of Jews) is beyond either the ability or the willingness of ethical people to accept.

In late 1944, however, Allied armies advancing toward the heart of Germany from both the east and the west began liberating tens of thousands of cadaver-like inmates of German concentration camps. All across Germany, liberating forces uncovered undeniable evidence of German efforts to eliminate the Jews. To the shock and dismay of the outside world, even the most contemptible rumors of German bestiality were revealed as truth. Once apprised of the horrendous truth, good people everywhere cried out for justice.

After liberation, survivors from Wobbelin concentration camp reveal the tragic circumstances they had to endure at the hands of the Nazis.

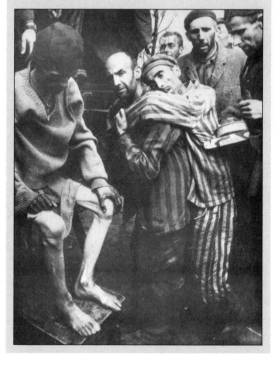

"God Bless America!"

Survivors of Dachau, one of the worst concentration camps, line the electric fence to welcome Allied soldiers. German atrocities against the Jews were revealed to the world when the Allies liberated Europe.

Much of the world did not learn of German atrocities against the Jews until Allied liberators swept across Europe in the final months of World War II. In *The Holocaust: A History of the Jews of Europe During World War II*, historian Martin Gilbert writes about the liberation of a group of Jewish survivors. Samuel Pisar, one of several teenage Jewish boys in hiding, recalled seeing the first Allied tanks and soldiers:

> I peeped through a crack in the wooden slats. Straight ahead, on the other side of the field, a huge tank was coming toward the barn. It stopped . . . . The tank's long cannon lofted its round head, as though peering at me, then turned slowly aside and let loose a tremendous belch. The firing stopped. The tank resumed its advance, lumbering cautiously toward me. I looked for the hateful swastika, but there wasn't one. On the tank's side, instead, I made out an unfamiliar emblem.

It was a five-pointed white star. In an instant, the realization flooded me; I was looking at the insignia of the United States army.

My skull seemed to burst. With a wild roar, I broke through the thatched roof, leaped to the ground, and ran toward the tank. . . . I was still running. I was in front of the tank, waving my arms. The hatch opened. A big black man climbed out, swearing unintelligibly at me. Recalling the only English I knew, those words my mother had sighed while dreaming of our deliverance, I fell at the black man's feet, threw my arms around his legs and yelled at the top of my lungs:

"God bless America!"

With an unmistakable gesture, the American motioned me to get up and lifted me through the hatch. In a few minutes, all of us were free.

The London Agreement

On May 8, 1945, Germany surrendered unconditionally. Victorious Allied leaders, pressured by world opinion, needed to move quickly to find a way of dealing with high-ranking Nazi war criminals. Despite a worldwide clamor to punish German offenders, especially those involved with maltreatment of the Jews, establishing their guilt became problematical.

Several top Nazis were already dead. Archcriminal Adolf Hitler, to avoid capture and certain punishment, had committed suicide on April 30, 1945. Propaganda minister Joseph Goebbels killed his family and himself in Hitler's Berlin bunker on May 1. Heinrich Himmler and Reinhard Heydrich, chief architects of the Final Solution, were also dead: Himmler by his own hand, Heydrich of wounds received from an assassin's bomb. Of the top Nazi Party leaders, only Reich Marshal Hermann Göring was in Allied custody.

Adding to the Allies' problems, existing international law provided no means for prosecuting war criminals. And Allied leaders could not agree on how to proceed in the absence of sound legal precedents. "The triumphant Allies came out of World War II flushed with victory," writes Snyder, "but divided upon virtually all policies except one: the German war criminals would be punished." With only a single thread to unite them, the Allies persevered until an accord was reached. Dr. Snyder goes on:

An agreement dated August 8, 1945, between the United States, Great Britain, and the Soviet Union [and France] to try the Nazi leaders was subsequently endorsed by nineteen member states of the United Nations. Although special courts had been set up in the past to judge political crimes by extraordinary authority, no such court had ever obtained universal recognition.[3]

The Four Power pact became known as the London Agreement. The pact comprised two parts: the Agreement proper, and the Charter. The Agreement called for the prosecution of war criminals before an International Military Tribunal (IMT); the Charter provided the constitution, jurisdiction, and functions of the tribunal.

The War Crimes Trials

In the broadest sense, Nazi war crimes can be separated into two types: crimes involving the organized looting of property and liquid assets, and crimes against individuals and targeted ethnic groups. The London Agreement's Charter further classified Nazi transgressions as crimes against peace, war crimes, and crimes against humanity.

In October 1945 the Allies brought formal charges against twenty-two major Nazi war criminals. Their collective trial commenced on November 20, 1945, in Nuremberg, Germany. Each of the principals was tried on at least two of four counts (derived from the foregoing three categories) as follows:

Count One: Common Plan or Conspiracy; plotting with others to wage wars of aggression in violation of international treaties, agreements, or assurances (as interpreted and determined by the Allies);

Count Two: Crimes Against Peace; planning, preparation, initiation, and waging wars of aggression;

Count Three: War Crimes; particularly those crimes involving the maltreatment

A scene from the Nuremberg trials shows some of the defendants in the case. While many people wanted to label the men tried at Nuremberg as sadistic and mentally ill, psychologists who studied the men found them to be, with rare exceptions, perfectly sane.

of prisoners of war in breach of international agreements;

Count Four: Crimes Against Humanity; such as murder, extermination, enslavement, deportation, and other inhumane acts against civilian populations.

The first Nuremberg trial lasted until October 1946. "The legality of the trial troubled many jurists who were disturbed by the ex post facto [after the fact] implications of the proceedings," Dr. Snyder notes. "As the proceedings went on and it became clear from the testimony what had happened in Nazi Germany, fewer voices were raised against the trial."[4]

The first Nuremberg proceedings, or what might be considered the first phase of the Nazi war crimes trials, laid a legal foundation for subsequent trials to build on. Between November 1946 and April 1949, a second phase of twelve separate trials held before U.S. military tribunals determined the fate of an additional 185 defendants.

Many other trials, conducted simultaneously with the second-phase trials or over the following decades, throughout Eastern and Central Europe and particularly in

Second-Phase Trials in Nuremberg

The trial of twenty-two major Nazi war criminals in Nuremberg from November 1945 to October 1946 laid the foundation for subsequent trials to build on. Between November 1946 and April 1949, U.S. Military Tribunals in Nuremberg presided over a second phase of war crimes trials conducted in twelve separate proceedings:

1. *Doctors Trial:* Twenty-three Nazi doctors tried for experiments conducted upon concentration camp inmates.

2. *Erhard Milch Trial:* Milch tried for crimes involving forced labor and medical experiments at Dachau.

3. *Jurists Trial:* Fifteen Nazi judges tried for abuses of the legal process within the Third Reich.

4. *Oswald Pohl Trial:* Eighteen members of the Economic and Administrative Main Office of the SS tried for crimes against forced laborers and concentration camp inmates.

5. *Friedrich Flick Trial:* Six industrialists tried for collusion in confiscating Jewish property and in using forced labor.

6. *I. G. Farben Trial:* Twenty-four members of the leading chemical company's board of directors tried for offenses similar to those cited in the Flick trial.

7. *Hostage Trial:* Twelve senior officers of the German army tried for maltreating civilians in southeastern Europe.

8. *RUSHA Trial:* Fourteen SS officers of the Race and Resettlement Office tried for involvement with policies of genocide.

9. *Einsatzgruppen Trial:* Twenty-four senior SS and SD officers tried as leaders of units responsible for mass murder.

10. *Krupp Trial:* Nineteen senior Krupp corporate officials tried for confiscating property and exploiting slave labor.

11. *Ministries Trial:* Twenty-one senior Nazi diplomats and governmental officials tried for various offenses related to implementing Hitler's racially supremacist New Order in Europe.

12. *Oberkommando Wehrmacht (OKW) Trial:* Fourteen members of the high command of the German army tried for crimes against prisoners of war and against civilians in occupied areas.

West Germany, constituted a third phase. This phase remains ongoing, as indicated by European journalist Gita Sereny, who writes: "Between 1958 and 1968, 150 major Nazi-crimes trials took place in the eleven *Länder* (states) of West Germany and they have continued ever since."[5]

Two major trials were also held in Israel. Adolf Eichmann, former head of the Jewish Affairs section of the Gestapo (*GEheime STAatsPOlizei*; secret state police), was tried in Jerusalem in 1961. And John Demjanjuk, accused of being the wicked "Ivan the Terrible," operator of the Treblinka gas chamber, stood trial during 1987–1988, also in Jerusalem.

Brutal Crimes and Normal Men

Over the past five decades, several thousand German war criminals have been held accountable for acts so despicable as to far exceed the limits of simple barbarity. Tens (perhaps hundreds) of thousands more have evaded proper punishment for their murderous deeds. Of those brought to trial, most were murderers of one kind or another. As historian Dr. Klaus B. Fischer puts it:

> There were two types of murderers—those who sat behind the desks and gave the orders—the desk murderers such as Hitler, Himmler, Heydrich, Müller, and Eichmann; and the men who carried out the actual executions or gassings—Höss, Wirth, Mengele, the men of the *Einsatzgruppen* ["task forces," or mobile killing squads], and the concentration camp guards.[6]

According to Dr. Fischer, their "crimes against people can be grouped into five broad categories: (1) slave labor, (2) abuse of prisoners of war, (3) torture and execution of hostages, (4) cruel and unusual medical experiments, and (5) organized atrocities."[7]

Given the heinous nature of the crimes, a reasonable person might readily conclude that most of the perpetrators were sadists. But the evidence indicates otherwise. Dr. Ella Lingens-Reiner, a physician who survived Auschwitz, observed:

> There were few sadists. Not more than five or ten percent were pathological criminals in

the clinical sense. The others were all perfectly normal men who knew the difference between right and wrong. They all knew what was going on.[8]

Discounting sadism as a prime motivator for these crimes, the answer to what would enable "perfectly normal men" to murder millions of people must reside in the larger cultural patterns in German society and in the institutional mechanisms of the state. Dr. Fischer suggests four patterns that existed in Nazi Germany:

Hitler sits at his desk, from which he orchestrated the deaths of over six million Jews.

(1) a virulent form of anti-Semitism with strong biological and religious components; (2) a powerful tradition of institutionalized authoritarianism in family, school, and everyday life; (3) belligerent nationalism based on lack of identity, insecurity, and the trauma of defeat in war; and (4) rule by a criminal leadership.[9]

The Germans varied the nature of their crimes with respect to the geographical location of the conquered territory and the ethnic makeup of the populace. Dr. Fischer cites the following examples:

Eastern and southeastern European countries were subjected to a far greater degree of inhumanity than the northern or western countries. The Nazis viewed the Scandinavians, Dutch, and Flemish as racial kinsmen who would eventually share dominance in the new German order. The populations living to the west and south of the Germanic people—the French, Spaniards, Italians— were considered to be of inferior racial quality but worthy of being potential allies. The eastern and southeastern peoples, on the other hand, were regarded as racially inferior and fit only to be slaves. The Poles, for example, were to be uprooted at will to make room for new Germanic settlers. The remainder of Poland was to be subjected to a policy of spoliation [plunder] that Hitler himself called the devil's work (*Teufelswerk*). In Poland, Russia, and the Balkan countries the German authorities plundered at will. Although the rest of Europe was not treated quite as shamelessly, the pattern was similar.[10]

In summary, then, Nazi war crimes were directed toward both people and properties; they were brutal in nature, varying in severity according to geographical location and population ethnicity; and, although some of the perpetrators profiled in the pages to follow were unquestionably sadists, most of the crimes were committed by ordinary Germans.

Annals of the Damned

The following chapters explore the lives of several leading Nazi war criminals and the roles they played in implementing the Final Solution to the Jewish question. Because so much has already been written about the life and crimes of Adolf Hitler and Nazi first deputy Hermann Göring, their names are excluded. As the top two Nazis, however, their roles are inextricably linked with those of their underlings. To that extent, they receive frequent mention in subsequent profiles.

In selecting six Nazi war criminals for closer scrutiny, priority was given to those whose collective contribution to the extinction of European Jewry represents as broad a range of evil as is possible to show within the limits of six short chapters. Some of their names will elicit instant familiarity; the names of others will scarcely raise a glint of recognition. But the names of all are scribed in blood in the annals of the damned.

Heinrich Himmler: Architect of Genocide

Many Nazi war criminals have gradually fallen out of notoriety and are now beyond either remembrance or recognition. To be sure, the name of Adolf Hitler is scribed high on history's roll of consummate evildoers and will probably remain so for eons to come. But the names, faces, and deeds of even Hitler's chief cohorts in crime are becoming less remembered and recognized in the waning days of the twentieth century. Yet, if remembrance holds the key to deterring catastrophic recurrences, humankind would do well to preserve in indelible infamy the name of Heinrich Himmler—the aptly titled "architect of genocide."[11]

"The Hard Decision"

On October 4, 1943, Heinrich Himmler— SS Reich leader and chief of the German police (*Reichsführer-SS und Chef der Deutschen Polizei*)—addressed a gathering of his Higher SS and Police Leaders (HSSPL) at Poznań, in west-central Poland. He spoke for three hours and ten minutes. Some two hours into his speech, he said in words styled fretfully, almost regretfully:

I also want to talk to you quite frankly on a very grave matter. Among ourselves it should be mentioned quite frankly and yet we will never speak of it publicly. . . . I mean the evacuations of the Jews, the extermination [*Ausrottung*] of the Jewish race. It is one of the things it is easy to talk about. "The Jewish race is being exterminated," says one party member, it is quite clear, it is our program—the elimination of Jews; and we are doing it, exterminating them. And then they come, eighty million worthy Germans, and each one has his decent Jews. Of course, the others are vermin, but this one is an "A1" Jew. Not one of those who talk this way has witnessed it, not one of them has been through it. Most of you must know what it means when a hundred corpses are lying side by side or five hundred or a thousand. To have stuck it out and at the same time—apart from exceptions caused by human weakness—to have remained decent men, that is what has made us hard. This is a page of glory in our history which has never been written and is never to be written.[12]

In his chronicle of the SS (*Schutzstaffel*, or protective force), historian Gerald Reitlinger asserts that the foregoing speech was "Himmler's one and only public allusion to the extermination of Jewry."[13] But several other historians have noted that Himmler spoke in a similar vein to a group of *Gauleiters* (district leaders) and *Reichsleiters* (Reich leaders) two days later. John Toland excerpts Himmler's second speech this way:

> The sentence "The Jews must be exterminated," with its few words, gentlemen, can be uttered easily. But what that sentence demands of the man who must execute it is the hardest and toughest thing in existence. . . . I ask you really only to hear and never to talk about what I tell you in this circle. When the question arose, "What should be done about the women and children?" I decided here to adopt a clear solution. I did not deem myself justified in exterminating the men, that is to say, to kill them or let them be killed, while allowing their children to grow up to avenge themselves on our sons and grandchildren. The hard decision had to be taken—*this people must disappear from the face of the earth*.[14]

And with that "hard decision" Heinrich Himmler guaranteed himself a permanent place in hell.

"Ophidian" Ways

From outward appearances, none would guess that Heinrich Himmler, the man chosen by Adolf Hitler to carry out the Final Solution, that is, the extermination of European Jewry, was a mass murderer. Walter Dornberger, the German rocket scientist responsible for developing the V-2 rocket used against Britain in World War II, once sat opposite him during an important briefing. He described Himmler as looking "like an intelligent elementary schoolteacher, certainly not a man of violence." Dornberger added the following impressions of the man who failed first as a fertilizer salesman and then as a chicken farmer before ascending to the heights of Nazi officialdom:

> I could not for the life of me see anything outstanding or extraordinary about this middle-sized, youthfully slender man in gray SS uniform. Under a brow of average height two gray-blue eyes looked out at me, behind glittering pince-nez [glasses], with an eye of peaceful interrogation. The trimmed moustache below the straight, well-shaped nose traced a dark line on his unhealthy pale features. The lips were

Heinrich Himmler justified the killing of women and children as the only way the Nazis could assure that children would not grow up to avenge their parents.

Adolf Hitler and Heinrich Himmler watch passing SS troops during Reich Party Day ceremonies in 1938. Hitler chose Himmler to directly implement the Final Solution.

colorless and very thin. Only the inconspicuous, receding chin surprised me. . . . His slender, pale and almost girlishly soft hands, covered with blue veins, lay motionless on the table throughout our conversation.[15]

An associate who knew Himmler more intimately—reputedly Felix Kersten, his masseur—described the SS leader's personality as "opaque, with something of the Japanese [inscrutability], rather than the European." Although "Himmler appeared to be easygoing, jovial, at peace with himself," his associate saw indications of the inner man:

His eyes were extraordinarily small, and the distance between them narrow, rodent-like. If you spoke to him, these eyes would never leave your face; they would rove over your countenance, fix your eyes; and in them would be an expression of waiting, watching, stealth. His manner of reacting to things which did not meet with his approval was also not quite that expected from the jovial bourgeois [middle-class person]. Sometimes his disagreement was clothed in the form of a fatherly admonition, but this could suddenly change and his speech and actions would become ironic, caustic, cynical. But never, even in these expressions of disagreement and dislike, did the man himself seem to appear. . . . Never any indication of directness. . . . Himmler[,] when fighting[,] intrigued[;] when battling for his so-called ideas used subterfuge, deceit—not dueling swords, but daggers in his opponent's back. His ways were the ophidian [snakelike] ways of the coward, weak, insincere and immeasurably cruel. . . . Himmler's mind . . . was not a twentieth century mind. His character was medieval, feudalistic, machiavellian, evil.[16]

The contrasting perceptions of Himmler noted by his contemporaries illuminate the complex character and paradoxical personality of the man. Belying the ordinary, scholarly appearance depicted by Dornberger, the very mention of Himmler's name struck terror in the hearts of millions of Europeans during the twelve-year reign of Germany's Third Reich. And more in keeping with Kersten's "ophidian" ways, Himmler, from a position of what many consider to be the second most powerful man in Nazi Germany, orchestrated the systematic destruction of many of those millions.

An Appetite for Activism

Born in Munich on October 7, 1900, Heinrich Himmler was the second of three sons produced by the union of Gebhard Himmler, a private tutor, and Anna Heyder Himmler, the daughter of a Bavarian tradesman. Not wealthy, but never in want, the Himmlers epitomized all that the term *bourgeois*, or middle class, embodies. Gebhard is generally described as having been devoutly Catholic and strictly authoritarian. These traits established the tenor of the Himmler household and carried over into every aspect of the children's upbringing.

While growing up, despite a sickly youth and a total lack of physical grace, Heinrich romanticized about becoming a soldier and pursuing a military career in the East. (Russia, he felt, represented both a threat to Germany's existence and an obsta-

cle in the path of Germany's future expansion.) He did, in fact, serve as an officer cadet with the Eleventh Bavarian Regiment toward the end of World War I. But he experienced only two weeks of action in September 1918 with No. 17 Machine Gun Company at Bayreuth on the western front.

After the war, he attended Munich Technical College and earned a degree in agriculture in 1922. While in school, he became active in various *Freikorps* (Free Corps)—nationalistic paramilitary groups calling for the elimination of "traitors to the Fatherland."[17] *Freikorps* groups consisted mainly of former officers and demobilized soldiers, right-wing extremists, military adventurers, and unemployed youths.

These groups scorned religion as a societal weakness and preached its abolition. Himmler, who much valued his Catholicism, soon found his religion in conflict with his militaristic aims. Even the dueling requirements of his student fraternity clashed with church doctrine. On December 15, 1919, Himmler wrote:

I believe I had come into conflict with my religion. Come what may, I shall always love God, shall pray to Him, shall remain faithful to the Catholic Church, and shall defend it even if I should be expelled from it.[18]

After taking his degree and working briefly as a fertilizer salesman, Himmler joined the *Reichskriegflagge* (German War Flag), another *Freikorps* group—this one headed by Ernst Röhm, a former German army officer and decorated war hero.

On November 8, 1923, under Röhm's leadership, the "owlish, bespectacled"[19] Himmler took part in the famous Beer Hall Putsch in Munich, Hitler's bungled attempt to overthrow the government of Germany's Weimar Republic by force. As Röhm's standard-bearer, Himmler did little more than show the *Reichskriegflagge* colors—an imperial German ensign—outside the War Ministry buildings in the center of Munich. But his small part in the failed putsch attracted the attention of some leading German nationalists and whetted his appetite for political activism.

A Loyal and Devoted Follower

Adolf Hitler and forty fellow conspirators, including Ernst Röhm, ended up in jail following the failed putsch in Munich. Hitler's Nazi Party (officially, *Nationalsozialistische Deutsche Arbeiterpartei* [NSDAP], or National Socialist German Workers' Party) was banned. Those who escaped punishment were forced to reorganize politically.

In 1924 Himmler, with the dissolution of his paramilitary group, found himself temporarily without a leader, out of uniform, and unemployed. He elected to join General Erich Ludendorff's National Socialist Freedom Movement, one of two *"völkisch"* ("pure German") groups that grew out of the banned Nazi Party. (The Nazi Party simply split into two factions with different names.)

For a time, Himmler served as secretary to Gregor Strasser, the past and future leader of the socialist wing of the Nazi Party and an early rival of Hitler's for overall party leadership. Under Strasser, Himmler became a wholly committed party propagandist, traveling about Lower Bavaria on a motorcycle, spreading the party message. "We do this hard work undeterred," he wrote. "It is a selfless service to a great idea and a great cause." [20]

It is uncertain as to when Himmler first met Hitler, but it is known that he became impressed with the future führer not long after Hitler's release from Landsberg prison. Hitler began at once reorganizing and revitalizing the Nazi Party. Shortly thereafter, Himmler's admiration for the man turned to adulation. Himmler later spoke of the early years of Hitler's rise to power as "glorious days," adding: "We members of the Movement were in constant danger of our lives, but we were not afraid. Adolf Hitler led us and held us together. They were the most wonderful years of my life." [21] Although the highly motivated Himmler craved power and possessed "intense self-discipline and organizing ability," [22] he lacked either the boldness or the imagination to rise to the level of the Hitlers and Stalins of the world. He required someone above him to guide him and to make the tough decisions. "Without direction," according to G. S. Graber, author and former editor of *European Digest*, "he was useless." [23]

In Adolf Hitler, Himmler had found the leader he so much needed. And in Heinrich Himmler, Hitler had gained a devoted and loyal follower.

The *Reichsführer-SS* Establishes Dominance

Loyalty in a subordinate was a quality that Hitler prized above all others. Nor did Himmler's organizing ability and hard work in promoting party objectives escape Hitler's watchful eye. Rewards for Himmler's industry and dedication came quickly. In 1925 he was appointed deputy *Gauleiter* (district leader) of Upper Bavaria and Swabia. Soon afterward he was named deputy Reich propaganda chief and, in 1927, deputy *Reichsführer-SS*.

Following his marriage to Margarethe Boden in 1928, Himmler and "Marga" bought a small farm at Waldtrudering, outside

NEW BRIGHTON HIGH SCHOOL
NEW BRIGHTON, PA 15066

Heinrich Himmler (right) shakes hands with Adolf Hitler at the führer's headquarters in this 1943 photo.

Munich. They bought fifty laying hens in an effort to turn the farm into a prospering chicken ranch. Marga bore Heinrich a daughter, Gudrun, in the first year of their marriage, their only child.

On January 6, 1929, Hitler appointed Himmler *Reichsführer-SS*. As the demands of his political career increased, Himmler began spending more and more time away from home. His extended absences resulted in the failure of the chicken ranch, and his relationship with Marga deteriorated into a marriage in name only. The couple began living apart. Politics and the pursuit of power consumed Himmler for the rest of his life.

Himmler waded into his new duties with characteristic energy and enthusiasm, at once proclaiming:

The SA [*Sturmabteilung*, storm detachment; popularly called storm troopers

or Brownshirts] is the infantry of the line, the SS the guards. There has always been a guard: the Persians had one, the Greeks, Caesar, Napoleon, and Frederick the Great, right up to the world war; the SS will be the imperial guard of the new Germany.[24]

Himmler, with swift efficiency, then proceeded to develop the SS from Hitler's personal bodyguard force of two hundred black-shirted troops into a formidable paramilitary unit and party weapon. Elected to the Reichstag (German parliament) as Nazi deputy for Weser-Ems in 1930, Himmler worked hard to build a state within a state. In June 1931, the tireless *Reichsführer-SS* warned:

Our enemies efforts to bolshevize [to make communist] Germany are increasing. Our information and intelligence service must aim to discover, and to suppress, our Jewish and Freemason enemies; this is the most important task of the SS today.[25]

At this point, spying became an obsession with the Nazis. To aid in the discovery of party enemies, Himmler assigned the task of building an intelligence service to Reinhard Heydrich.

The blond, blue-eyed Heydrich represented a towering example of Nordic racial purity to Himmler, who was about to become the Nazis' chief agent for German racial purification. Heydrich, a ruthless, intellectual opportunist, established the intelligence agency that ultimately grew into the *Sicherheitsdienst* (SD)—the SS Security Service. The two men then worked together diligently to ensure the Nazis' consolidation of power in Bavaria.

By 1933, *Reichsführer-SS* Himmler had swelled the ranks of the SS to some fifty-three thousand strong and had established its dominance in every sphere of state security and domestic policy.

The New Knights of Teuton

Himmler brought two indelible mind-sets to his role as chief of the SS: He held totally to the belief of a "mystic relation between blood and soil";[26] and he "was obsessed with the Nordic ideal, with dreams of racial purification for all SS men."[27]

Of his belief in a blood-soil relationship, he once wrote, "The yeoman [small farmer] on his own acre is the backbone of the German people's strength and character."[28] His degree in agriculture and his subsequent purchase of a small farm attested to his belief that superior blood strains lie rooted in the soil.

Reinhard Heydrich epitomized the Nazi ideal of Aryan manhood—tall, blond, blue-eyed, intelligent, and totally ruthless.

Louts Need Not Apply

The selection process for SS candidates stressed purity of racial background. *Reichsführer-SS* Heinrich Himmler required every SS applicant to submit a photograph with his application so that it might be examined for racial characteristics. In *Himmler: Reichsführer-SS*, Peter Padfield writes, "With young men appearance (*Aussehen*) counted above all." Padfield cites the following example excerpted from an early instruction from Himmler to his SS-Führers (SS leaders) in Munich:

A typical Slav-face would scarcely be taken in to the SS by an SS-Führer, because he [the Slav] would very soon notice that he had no community of blood [*Blutsgemeinschaft*] with his comrades of more Nordic origin. The photographs which have to accompany the application form serve the purpose of allowing the faces of the candidates to be seen at headquarters [the offices of the *Reichsleitung*, or Reich Leadership, in Munich]. . . . [I]n general we want only good fellows, not louts [*nur Kerle und keine Scheissherle*].

To Himmler, the land yielded a people's moral fiber and toughness; conversely, the cities spawned decadence and greed—and all else that was morally wrong with a society. Since significant numbers of Germany's Jews resided in cities and towns—as opposed to rural areas—Himmler easily made the transition from one who initially only selectively disliked *some* Jews to one who finally, indiscriminately, hated *all* Jews.

Long before his ascension to *Reichs-führer-SS*, Himmler had disavowed the Catholicism of his parents and youth. He retained admiration for the strictly disciplined monastic orders of his earlier religion, however, and patterned many of the ritualistic trappings of his SS on the tenets of the Order of Jesuits. Out of such discipline and ritual, he hoped to fashion his SS men into a modern knightly order, similar to the religiously fanatic Teutonic knights of the twelfth century.

Himmler envisioned the objective of his reborn knights as the protection of the Nordic German society from invasive, impure bloodlines of such perceived inferiors as Jews and Slavic people. In June 1931 he spoke about "the purpose and goal of the SS" to a convention of SS leaders in Berlin. He said that the selection of SS candidates was to be predicated not on size, as with earlier elite orders, but on race:

> For us, standing sublime above all doubt, it is the blood carrier who can make history; the Nordic race is decisive not only for Germany, but for the whole world.
>
> Should we succeed in establishing this Nordic race again from and around Germany and inducing them to become farmers, and from this seedbed producing a race of 200 million, then the world will belong to us. Should Bolshevism win, it will signify the extermination [*Austilgen*] of the Nordic race . . . devastation, the end of the world. . . . We are called, therefore, to create a basis on which the next generation can make history.[29]

As Hitler and the Nazis moved closer to attaining absolute power in Germany, *Reichsführer-SS* Himmler and his new Teutonic knights stood ready to sally forth in defense of Nordic purity.

"A Vast Machine of Political Oppression"

On January 30, 1933, Weimar president Paul von Hindenburg appointed Adolf Hitler as Germany's new chancellor. Hitler promptly installed his trusted followers in key positions, appointing Heinrich Himmler Munich police president and soon thereafter commander of all political police units outside Prussia. Within two months after Hitler assumed political power, all semblance of democratic government disappeared in Germany.

Notably, while in Munich and acting on Hitler's orders, Himmler established the first concentration camp in nearby Dachau, to incarcerate political enemies of the state. The camp opened on March 22, 1933. In a press release, Himmler announced:

> Here the entire communist and—so far as is necessary—Reichsbanner [unarmed private army of trade union workers] and Marxist officials who endanger the security of the state will be concentrated because it is not possible in the long run to hold individual communists in prison without overburdening the state machinery, and on the other hand it is equally impossible to allow these officials their freedom again.[30]

A camp network of staggering numbers—estimated by historian Daniel Jonah Goldhagen at more than ten thousand—followed the precedent set at Dachau, with the range of those qualifying for internment greatly extended. Hitler tasked Himmler with providing guard units for the camp system, which led to the creation of the feared SS Death's Head Formations (*SS-Totenkopfverbände*),

Himmler's "Engagement and Marriage Decree"

In establishing the SS, *Reichsführer* Heinrich Himmler envisioned more than just a new breed of racially pure Teutonic knights. "Since the object was not merely the establishment of an elite guard, but the provision of a seedbed of pure Nordic stock to spread through and reinvigorate the whole German nation," writes Peter Padfield in *Himmler: Reichsführer-SS*, "it was axiomatic that SS wives had to pass the same selection procedures as the men. Accordingly on 31 December 1931 . . . Himmler promulgated an 'Engagement and Marriage Decree.'

1. The SS is an association of German men of Nordic determination selected on special criteria.

2. In conformity with the National Socialist *Weltanschauung* [worldview] and recognizing that the future of our people depends on the selection and retention of racially and hereditarily sound good blood, I establish with effect from 1 January 1932 the 'marriage consent' for all unmarried members of the SS.

3. The goal striven for is the hereditarily sound, valuable extended family [*Sippe*] of German, Nordically determined type.

4. Marriage consent will be granted and denied solely and exclusively on the criteria of race and hereditary health.

5. Every SS man who intends to marry has to apply for this purpose to the Reichsführer-SS for the marriage consent.

6. SS members who marry despite having been denied the marriage consent will be dismissed from the SS; they will be given the option of resigning.

7. The appropriate processing of marriage requests is the task of the Race Office of the SS.

8. The Race Office of the SS manages the 'Clanbook of the SS' [*Sippenbuch der SS*], in which the families of the SS members will be entered after the granting of the marriage consent or approval of the request for registration.

9. The Reichsführer-SS, the head of the Race Office and the specialist of this office are bound to secrecy on their word of honor.

10. The SS is clear that with this order it has taken a step of great significance. Derision, scorn and misunderstanding do not affect us; the future belongs to us.

Heinrich Himmler"

later renowned for their brutal treatment of camp prisoners.

On April 20, 1934, Hitler, with Göring's approval, named Himmler to head the Prussian police and the Gestapo. Barely more than two months later, Himmler reached the turning point in his career. Hitler had become apprehensive over the growing threat to his leadership posed by Ernst Röhm, commander of the powerful SA, and Gregor Strasser, leader of the liberal wing of the Nazi Party. He called on Himmler and his SS to remove the threat.

Himmler accommodated his führer by masterminding and participating in a blood purge that commenced on the night of June

A view of the Dachau concentration camp shows the barracks where Jews were housed. The first concentration camp, Dachau was opened on March 22, 1933.

29–30, now widely known as the Night of the Long Knives (*Die Nacht der langen Messer*). During the purge, at least seventy-seven top Nazis—including Himmler's former mentors Röhm and Strasser—and about a hundred others were slain. The purge secured Hitler's grip on absolute power in Germany and guaranteed Himmler a favored place in the inner circle of Nazidom.

On June 17, 1936, Hitler ratified a decree unifying the German police for the first time in history and assigning Himmler the new title of "Reichsführer SS and Chief of the German Police in the Ministry of the Interior."[31] Himmler, having assumed total control of Germany's political and criminal police, now sat in the driver's seat of "a vast machine of political oppression."[32]

The Men of Himmler's SS

On September 1, 1939, Hitler sent his armies into Poland, thereby initiating World War II. The outbreak of war found Himmler at the pinnacle of his political power, but he continued to acquire new titles and responsibilities. A führer decree issued on October 5 appointed him Reichs

Himmler's Fountain of Life

Adolf Hitler, führer of Germany's Third Reich, intended to bring the German population up to a quality and quantity of 120 million Aryans—pureblooded Nordic types—by 1980. *Reichsführer-SS* Heinrich Himmler initiated extraordinary measures to meet Hitler's population goals. In *The Nazis*, historian Robert Edwin Herzstein and the editors of Time-Life Books depict some of the population inducements introduced by Himmler:

> Himmler's concern over population growth led him to conceive a new program, the Lebensborn, or Fountain of Life, and also to form a new bureau [Central Office for Race and Resettlement] to run the enterprise under his close supervision. "My first aim in setting up the Lebensborn," he later explained, "was to meet a crying need and give unmarried women who were actually racially pure a chance to have children free of cost."

> Toward this end, the bureau established a network of SS "homes," many of them in houses and hospitals that had been confiscated from the Jews. (Cynical Germans called the homes breeding farms and SS officers' clubs.) SS men would send their pregnant women friends there to have their children. . . .

> Himmler and the Lebensborn executives worked in concert with state ministries and party leaders to persuade young German women that they were "racially valuable" and should have offspring out of wedlock—a "biological marriage," it

was called—in order to satisfy the Reich's "urgent need for the victory of the German child."

> Simultaneously, the *Reichsführer-SS* campaigned vigorously against any practice that contravened a higher birth rate: contraception, abortion, the possession of pets ("Those who give a dog the place to which a child is entitled commit a crime against our people") and that darkest crime against Germanhood, homosexuality. Himmler was so adamant about homosexuals that he had his own errant nephew—an SS officer to boot—put to death in Dachau. He denied promotion to childless SS officers and enthusiastically backed a new law in 1938 that made a childless marriage grounds for divorce. (It apparently never occurred to Himmler that the SS man, rather than his woman, might be infertile.)

> Himmler was appalled to think of the damage that a war would do to Germany's genetic pool; warriors, the best breeding stock, might die in such numbers as to jeopardize the future of the German race. . . . He ordered SS men [when World War II came] to get their wives with child—and if possible to serve as "conception assistants" to childless women of 30 or older—before they put themselves in mortal peril. He gave the men generous leaves in which to perform their patriotic procreative duty. He urged idealistic German women to consummate biological marriages—"not in frivolity but in deep moral earnestness."

Commissar for the Consolidation of German Nationhood (*Reichskommissar für die Festigung deutschen Volkstums*). His new appointment entailed three principal duties: (1) the repatriation of ethnic Germans from abroad, initially from the Baltic states, then under Soviet jurisdiction; (2) "the elimination of the damaging influence of such portions of the foreign population as constitute a danger for the Reich and the German community"[33]—which implied continuing existing policies for eliminating Polish leaders and Jews in general; and (3) the establishment of new settlement areas for both repatriated Germans and those living in the Reich.

In carrying out his new duties, Himmler unleashed the power of special SS mobile killing squads, known as *Einsatzgruppen* (task forces). To oversee their sinister operations, he created the Reich Central Security Office (*Reichssicherheitshauptamt*, or RSHA) under the direction of Reinhard Heydrich. Heydrich, who had already established the first ghettos in Poland, also became the first administrator of concentration camps.

Heydrich's black-uniformed killing squads swept across eastern Europe like a plague, spreading political and anti-Semitic terror everywhere they went. For his part in enthusiastically planning and presiding over their activities—such as, espionage, the mass deportations of Jews and others to ghettos and concentration camps, torture, murder, and the systematic destruction of entire national and ethnic groups—Himmler laid a most well deserved claim to the title of "architect of genocide."

The genocide of Europe's Jews—the Final Solution—entered its final, destructive phase when the Germans invaded the Soviet Union on June 22, 1941. Three months earlier, Hitler had empowered Himmler to carry out "*special tasks . . .* entailed by the final

Heinrich Himmler (center) and Reinhard Heydrich (second from right) meet with other SS officials during World War II. Himmler appointed Heydrich to head the Reich Central Security Office.

SS troops in formation at Nuremberg in 1938. These troops were used to round up Jews and send them to concentration camps.

struggle that will have to be carried out between two opposing political systems." In Hitler-speak, "special tasks" meant the mass murder of Jews in the eastern areas targeted for invasion. Hitler further authorized Himmler to "act independently [of the German army] and on his own responsibility."[34]

In the summer of 1941, newly recruited and trained units of *Einsatzgruppen* followed the German army into the Soviet Union with orders to eliminate the "Judeo-

Bolshevik threat"[35]—that is, to kill Jews and Communists. During their first sweep, victims were marched to execution sites, ordered to undress, then killed by gunfire. Some six hundred thousand victims had been summarily executed this way by November 1941.

Psychological disturbances suffered by many of the *Einsatzgruppen* killers led to changes in operational procedures. Killing methods were revised to include the use of

A Lifelong Shock

In 1941, Heinrich Himmler conducted an inspection tour of *Einsatzgruppen* operations behind the eastern front. In *The Holocaust*, Martin Gilbert recounts SS general Karl Wolff's recollections of Himmler, who "asked to see a shooting operation." His recollection follows:

An open grave had been dug and they had to jump into this and lie face downwards. And sometimes when one or two rows had already been shot, they had to lie on top of the people who had already been shot and then they were shot from the edge of the grave. And Himmler had never seen dead people before and in his curiosity he stood right up at the edge of this open grave . . . and was looking in.

While he was looking in, Himmler had the deserved bad luck that from one or other of the people who had been shot in the head he got a splash of brains on his coat, and I think it also splashed into his face, and he went very green and pale; he wasn't actually sick, but he was heaving and turned round and swayed and then I had to jump forward and hold him steady and then I led him away from the grave.

After the shooting was over, Himmler gathered the shooting squad in a semi-circle around him and, standing up in his car, so that he would be a little higher and be able to see the whole unit, he made a speech. He had seen for himself how hard the task which they had to fulfill for Germany in the occupied areas was, but however terrible it all might be, even for him as a mere spectator, and how much worse it must be for them, the people who had to carry it out, he could not see any way round it.

Heinrich Himmler addresses SS troops on the eastern front.

Prisoners load the bodies of their comrades on a truck at Dachau. The corpses are so emaciated that they hardly look human.

gas vans and, eventually, fixed extermination camps at Belzec, Sobibor, Treblinka, Chelmno, Majdanek, and Auschwitz-Birkenau.

Of the more than six million Jews murdered during the Holocaust, most historians believe that *Einsatzgruppen* and police units killed about two million. Most of the other victims died in the gas chambers of the aforementioned death camps—administrated, staffed, and run by the men of Himmler's SS.

No Kinder Fate

After the invasion of the Soviet Union, Himmler controlled the administration of the newly occupied territories. Over the next two years, he expanded the SS from three to thirty-five divisions, until it approached parity with the German army itself.

Appointed minister of the interior in August 1943, Himmler tightened his hold on civil services and the courts to curb a growing defeatism in Germany. At the same time, he expanded the concentration camps and the death camps, organized the flow and utilization of expendable forced labor, and authorized bizarre medical experiments in the camps.

In August 1944, with the tide of war already beginning to turn in favor of the

Captured elderly members of the Völkssturm, *or People's Army, who were to defend Berlin. Himmler was also in charge of this army, made up of mostly young adults and the elderly.*

Allies, Hitler placed Himmler in command of the *Völkssturm* (People's Army). The *Völkssturm*, comprising mostly boys and old men, was charged with the defense of Berlin. With this appointment, Himmler's power was exceeded only by Hitler's.

In November 1944, in the face of advancing Russian troops, Himmler ordered the crematoria at Auschwitz destroyed, followed by the mass evacuation of Jews from the camp vicinity. Long death marches (*Todesmarsche*) commenced, as camp inmates were relocated. Approximately one hundred thousand Jews died or were

gunned down during these evacuations, which continued all winter.

In early 1945 Hitler named Himmler to head the *Werwölfe*, a last-ditch defense unit under orders to defend Germany to the last man in the Bavarian mountains. But Himmler could see Germany's Third Reich crumbling around him and began thinking more in terms of his own personal safety. With the realization that Germany could no longer win the war, Himmler's loyalty and devotion to his beloved führer finally waned.

In April Himmler called a halt to the Final Solution and sent out peace feelers to the Allies through a Swedish neutralist, offering to negotiate a German capitulation and to release Jews from concentration and death camps as a show of good faith. The Allies rejected his overtures.

Hitler, furious at his *Reichsführer*'s betrayal, ordered Himmler's arrest and execution. But Himmler surrounded himself with an SS entourage and put himself out of immediate reach, thus avoiding Hitler's wrath.

On April 29, 1945, Hitler, having decided to end his life, issued his last testament. With regard to Himmler, he wrote: "Before my death I expel from the Party and from all his offices the former Reichsführer-SS and Reich Interior Minister, Heinrich Himmler."[36] Hitler took his own life by pistol shot on the following day.

The Germans surrendered unconditionally to the Allies on May 8, 1945. By disguising himself and using the credentials of a dead German soldier, Himmler delayed his arrest by Allied forces for two weeks. Troops of Britain's Second Army finally took him into custody at Bremervörde, northeast of Bremen.

On May 23, 1945, while undergoing an examination by a British medical officer, Himmler bit down on a vial of potassium cyanide that he had concealed in a gap between his teeth. He died twelve minutes later.

In such ignominy ended the sordid career of *Reichsführer-SS* Heinrich Himmler, whom renowned social philosopher and psychoanalyst Erich Fromm once described as "an example of the sadistic authoritarian who developed a passion for unlimited control over others."[37] If left to his captors, one might safely conclude, no kinder fate awaited the "architect of genocide."

2 Julius Streicher: "Jew-Baiter Number One"

Julius Streicher was the consummate anti-Semite and a master rabble-rouser for the Nazi Party. Often described by both his peers and historians as cruel, sadistic, and corrupt, he proudly called himself "Jew-baiter number one."[38] And throughout his adulthood he strove to live up to his self-imposed appellation.

Born the son of a schoolteacher on February 12, 1885, in the Upper Bavarian village of Fleinhausen, Streicher followed his father's lead and chose teaching as a profession. Little is known of his early life except that he taught in a primary school in 1909 in a Nuremberg suburb. During World War I he served with a Bavarian unit. Overcoming an early reprimand for bad behavior, he went on to earn a commission as lieutenant and two decorations for bravery (the Iron Cross, First and Second Classes).

In 1919 Streicher returned to civilian life and resumed his schoolteaching career in Nuremberg. He soon became involved in politics and founded the anti-Semitic German Socialist Party (*Deutschsozialistische Partei*), which he merged with the Nazi Party in 1921. Two years later he founded *Der Stürmer* (*The Storm*), a sleazy newspaper that he used primarily to monger hatred for the Jews. Lest there be any doubt as to its reason for existence, the banner headline of *Der Stürmer* featured the slogan "The Jews Are Our Misfortune."[39]

Streicher's published anti-Semitic rantings soon caught the eye of Adolf Hitler, who read each issue of *Der Stürmer* from cover to cover. Streicher, as leader of the German Socialist Party, had been one of Hitler's early political rivals. But Hitler now saw him as a potentially valuable propaganda tool. Hitler was quick to reach out to anyone who could be of use to him. According to William L. Shirer, foreign correspondent and chronicler of Nazi Germany, "Murderers, pimps, homosexual perverts, drug addicts or just plain rowdies were all the same to him if they served his purpose."[40] Streicher, who likely felt himself in good company, was delighted to join Hitler's growing aggregation of fawning misfits and blind followers.

As a rabid racist and one of the earliest Nazis in Bavaria, he was welcomed into the circle of Hitler's most intimate friends. From 1922 until 1939, Streicher retained Hitler's favor, baiting Jews and inciting hatred and violence in the pages of *Der Stürmer*, until, writes Shirer, "his star finally faded."[41]

Conduct Unbecoming

Streicher, a bald, neckless, sexually sadistic agitator, always carried a whip and derived

Hitler and Julius Streicher (right of center), together at a German Day Rally in Nuremberg in 1933. Streicher's hatred of the Jews allowed him to become one of Hitler's most intimate friends.

enormous pleasure in pummeling helpless victims in the presence of others. Notable historian John Toland sketches the following portrait of Streicher:

> A stocky, primitive man with bald head and gross features, he gave off an aura of raw energy. He had excessive appetites alike at table and in bed. He could be bluffly jovial or blatantly brutal, shifting effortlessly from maudlin sentimentality to ruthlessness. Like Hitler, he was rarely seen in public without a whip but where the former draped his from the wrist like a dog leash, Streicher flaunted his like a weapon. In younger days he had "restlessly wandered from place to place with a rucksack full of anti-Semitic books and pamphlets." His speech was glutted with sadistic imagery and he relished attacking personal enemies in the foulest terms. Convinced that the Jew was plotting against the Aryan world, he had an endless catalogue of abuse at the tip of his tongue.[42]

Shirer, who spent several years in Germany just prior to World War II, describes Streicher as "a noted pervert and one of the most unsavory characters in the Third Reich."[43] Klaus P. Fischer, who joins Shirer as an astute recorder of Nazi Germany's history, depicts Streicher as "a sexual deviate and a bully." Fischer further observes: "It has been suggested that the leering, sexually obsessed Jew he conjured up in the pages of *Der Stürmer* was really a reflection of his own conduct, a form of conduct that was by most standards crude and uncivilized."[44]

Yet it was through Streicher's unrestrained crudity in the pages of *Der Stürmer* that he accrued personal wealth and gained favor, not only with Hitler and his Nazi colleagues but among the masses of ordinary Germans. It was also that same crudeness that ultimately offended even the Nazis and toppled him from grace. Meanwhile, for some eighteen years, Streicher enjoyed a place of prominence in Hitler's hierarchy and played a dominant role in instilling the Nazi canon of bigotry and racism in the malleable minds of millions of Germans.

In 1925 Streicher was named *Gauleiter* (district leader) of Franconia (a duchy in southeast Germany) for the Nazi Party, with headquarters in Nuremberg. Soon afterward he began experiencing difficulties in his teaching position. Louis L. Snyder tells us:

He insisted that his pupils greet him each day with *"Heil Hitler!"* He continually denounced the government of the Weimar Republic [Germany's govern-

A photo of Streicher's virulently anti-Semitic Der Stürmer. *The paper was popular with Nazis and ordinary Germans.*

ment before the Nazis rose to power] and on one occasion took sick leave to attend a Nazi rally in Munich. In 1928, charges were brought against him, and he was dismissed for conduct unbecoming a teacher. Later he expressed great pride in this "achievement."[45]

Already financially secure from his earnings as *Der Stürmer*'s publisher, Streicher's dismissal as a teacher simply allowed him more time to devote to politics and muckraking. And for the next seventeen years, he set a new standard for personal repulsiveness and "conduct unbecoming."

Streicher's "Idealism"

In 1929 Streicher was elected to the Bavarian legislature (Landtag) as a Nazi delegate from Franconia. As the Nazis surged into power in January 1933, he won election to the Reichstag as a Nazi delegate from Franconia. At the same time Hitler appointed him to head the Central Committee for Counteracting Jewish Atrocity Tales and Boycott Propaganda. A year later he was promoted to lieutenant general in the SS (*SS-Gruppenführer*).

Much of Streicher's "political influence," according to author and historian Robert S. Wistrich, "derived from the impact of *Der Stürmer*." Writes Wistrich:

This weekly newspaper became the world's best known anti-semitic publication with its crude cartoons, repellent photographs of Jews, its stories of ritual murder, pornography and its coarse prose style. Through its columns and through his own endless speaking tours, Streicher reached millions of Germans, imbuing them with his own poisonous

A kiosk advertising Streicher's Der Stürmer *carries the motto, "The Jews are our misfortune. Read* Der Stürmer *against Jews."*

brew of hatred, sadism and perversity. The impact of *Der Stürmer* was greatly enhanced by a nationwide system of display cases (*Stürmerkasten*) put up in parks, public squares, factory canteens, at street corners and bus stops, to attract passersby. Their visual impact, their racist slogans and scandalmongering style drew crowds. *Der Stürmer* consistently carried large print slogans such as "Avoid Jewish Doctors and Lawyers," and gave listings of Jewish dentists, shopkeepers and professional people whom "Aryans" were urged to avoid. Those who ignored this advice were in danger of having their own names and addresses listed.[46]

A recurring theme of Streicher's scandal sheet decried the violation of golden-haired German maidens by swarthy, impure, and invariably rich Jewish lechers:

> One single cohabitation of a Jew with an Aryan woman is sufficient to poison her blood forever. Never again will she be able to bear purely Aryan children, even when married to an Aryan. They will all be bastards.
>
> Now we know why the Jew uses every artifice of seduction in order to ravish German girls at as early an age as is possible; why the Jewish doctor rapes his female patients while they are under anesthetic.[47]

Hitler relished Streicher's material and denied repeated requests to curtail publication of *Der Stürmer* as a "cultural disgrace."[48] Apparently much of the German populace shared Hitler's enjoyment of Streicher's smut, as *Der Stürmer*'s circulation increased from 2,000 to 3,000 in 1923 to 65,000 in 1934, and peaked in 1940 at about 600,000. Hitler surprised critics of Strei-

Words into Action

"In the pages of *Der Stürmer* there constantly appeared slanders against the Jews," writes Whitney R. Harris, a former assistant prosecutor at the proceedings in Nuremberg during 1945–1946. In his book *Tyranny on Trial*, Harris includes Julius Streicher's self-stated purpose for attacking the Jews in print:

> The continued work of *Der Stürmer* will help to ensure that every German down to the last man will, with heart and hand, join the ranks of those whose aim it is to crush the head of the serpent Pan-Juda [all Jews] beneath their heels. He who helps bring this about helps to eliminate the devil, and the devil is the Jew.

Harris offers the following excerpts from articles published by Streicher during the first two years of the war:

> September, 1939: "The Jewish people ought to be exterminated root and branch. Then the plague of pests would have disappeared in Poland also at one stroke."
>
> February, 1940: "At the end of this Jewish war the extermination of the Jewish people will have been brought about."
>
> March, 1940: "The Jew is a devil in human form. It is fitting that he be exterminated root and branch."
>
> November, 1940: "The Jewish rabble will be exterminated like the weeds and vermin so that it can never again disturb the bloodily fought for peace of the European peoples."

cher's grievous exaggerations with an unexpected response: "The truth is the opposite of what people say: he *idealized* the Jew. The Jew is baser, fiercer, more diabolical than Streicher depicted him."[49]

The Wings of Greed

Streicher's part in creating the hostile mindset that prevailed in Nazi Germany that led to—and sanctioned—the Final Solution is difficult to measure. At the very least, his contribution to the destruction of Europe's Jews was enormous.

As early as April 3, 1925, Streicher called for the annihilation of Jews: "For thousands of years the Jews have been destroying peoples; make a beginning today so that we can destroy the Jews."[50] On April 1, 1933, he headed a boycott against Jewish shops and offices, officially proclaimed as an act of reprisal for Jewish claims of Nazi brutalities. That same day he delivered a speech—typical of many more to follow—outlining the premises of the newly empowered Nazi regime's anti-Semitic program:

> Never since the beginning of the world and the creation of man has there been a nation which dared to fight against the nation of bloodsuckers and extortioners who, for a thousand years, have spread all over the world. . . . It was left to our [Nazi] Movement to expose the Jew as a mass murderer. . . . As long as I stand at the head of the struggle, this struggle will be conducted so honestly that the eternal Jew will derive no joy from it.[51]

As the circulation of *Der Stürmer* increased, so too did Streicher's vitriol.

He championed a nationwide smear campaign against the Jews that led to the adoption of the Nuremberg Laws of 1935—the infamous laws that stripped the Jews of their rights and citizenship in Germany—at a rally staged by him that year in Nuremberg. And in 1937, he warned: "The Jew always lives from the blood of other peoples; he needs murders and sacrifices. Victory will only be achieved when the whole world is free of Jews."[52]

On November 10, 1938, in Nuremberg, Streicher spoke out in public support of the

Hitler (in street, giving Nazi salute) along with Göring, Streicher, and others. Streicher's virulent anti-Semitism ensured him a position of power in the Nazi elite.

nationwide pogrom (organized massacre) then being conducted against the Jews. (The pogrom—later known as *Kristallnacht*, or the Night of Broken Glass—was staged by the Nazis, allegedly in retaliation for the assassination of a minor German diplomat in Paris by a seventeen-year-old Jewish boy.) Streicher used the Nazi rampage and his position as *Gauleiter* to turn a tidy profit. In describing Streicher's role in the pogrom, historians Anthony Read and David Fisher write:

> Old-fashioned, gangster-style extortion was also practiced on a considerable scale. A number of Jews reported that they had been forced to sign over their property at a tenth of its value or less, on pain of death. . . .
>
> By November 14, the local party [under Streicher's leadership] had acquired much of the Jewish property in Nuremberg—569 pieces of land and buildings were recorded as being sold in under a month. These included a synagogue worth in excess of 100,000 Reichsmarks [RM] sold for RM100. It was later estimated that the difference between the real value and the sale value of all the property Streicher and his cronies had acquired amounted to a staggering 21 million Reichsmarks ($8.4 million).[53]

As 1938 ended, Streicher was flying high on the wings of greed and ill-gotten gains, but what goes up must inevitably observe the laws of gravity. "Ironically, the pogrom was to be the principal cause of Streicher's fall from power," Read and Fisher contend. "He had simply become too greedy and had not bothered to use any of his Jewish windfall to buy off his masters in Berlin."[54]

Decline of a Demagogue

In Shirer's words, Streicher's "star finally faded" in 1940. By then, in the face of countless complaints lodged against Streicher, even Hitler had grown weary of trying to justify his disciple's churlish conduct. Many of the complaints came from the arch-Jew-baiter's fellow Nazis. Streicher loved to boast of his amorous conquests and even more loved to belittle the virility of many of his comrades. But Streicher opened his filthy mouth once too often when he set in motion the rumor that Hermann Göring "was impotent and that his daughter, Edda, had been conceived by artificial insemination." Streicher apologized to the number-two Nazi later but the damage had been done. "Göring retaliated by sending a commission to Franconia to examine Streicher's business activities. As a result, Streicher was dismissed from his party posts in 1940."[55]

On November 23, 1940, Berlin correspondent Shirer added the following entry in his journal:

> I hear from party circles that Julius Streicher, the sadistic, Jew-baiting czar of Franconia and notorious editor of the anti-Semitic weekly [*Der*] *Stürmer*, has been arrested on orders of Hitler. No tears will be shed within or without the party, for he was loathed by nearly all. I shall always remember him swaggering through the streets of Nuremberg, where he was absolute boss, brandishing the riding whip which he always carried. He has been arrested, say party people, pending investigation of certain financial matters. If Hitler cared much, he could make some additional investigations. He could look into the little matter of how it came about that so many party leaders acquired great country estates and castles.[56]

Hitler, of course, cared little about real estate acquisitions. And rather than imprisoning Streicher, Hitler allowed him to spend the rest of the war on his farm. The demagogue "loathed by nearly all" continued to spew his venom in *Der Stürmer* until 1943.

"Purim Fest, 1946"

Streicher was indicted by the International Military Tribunal after the war for crimes against peace and crimes against humanity and tried in Nuremberg—the city that had formerly served as his headquarters. On October 1, 1946, the tribunal returned with the following judgment (shown in part) against Streicher:

> For his 25 years of speaking, writing, and preaching hatred of the Jews, Streicher was widely known as "Jew-Baiter Number 1." In his speeches and articles, week after week, month after month, he infected the German mind with the virus of anti-Semitism, and incited the German people to active persecution. [The judgment went on to note Streicher's culpability in staging the Jewish boycott in April 1933; his advocacy of the Nuremberg Laws of 1935; his responsibility for the destruction of a Jewish synagogue in Nuremberg in August 1938; and his public support of the nationwide Jewish pogrom in November 1938.] But it was not only in Germany that this defendant advocated his doctrines. As early as 1938 he began to call for the extermination of the Jewish race. . . . With knowledge of the extermination of the Jews in the Occupied Eastern Territories, this defendant continued to write and publish his propaganda of death. . . . Streicher's incitement to murder and extermination at the time when Jews in the East were being killed under the most horrible conditions clearly constitutes persecution on political and racial grounds in connection with war crimes, as defined by the [IMT] Charter, and constitutes a crime against humanity.[57]

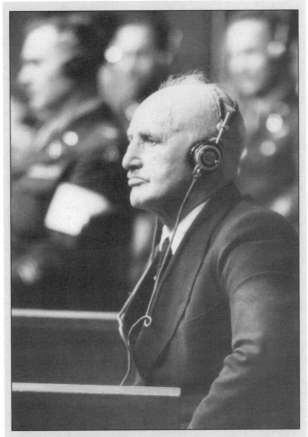

Defendant Julius Streicher on the witness stand during the Nuremberg trials. Streicher was found guilty of crimes against humanity.

The tribunal absolved Streicher of crimes against peace but found him guilty of crimes

"Stamp of Dishonor"

The defendants who stood in judgment before the International Military Tribunal in Nuremberg after World War II were allowed to make a final unsworn statement in their own behalf. In *The Anatomy of the Nuremberg Trials*, Telford Taylor, the former U.S. assistant chief prosecutor at Nuremberg, extracted Julius Streicher's statement:

> The prosecution had asserted that mass killings [of Jews] could not have been possible without Streicher and his [*Der*] *Stürmer*. The prosecution neither offered nor submitted any proof of this assertion. . . .
>
> These actions of the leader of the State [Hitler] against the Jews can be explained by the attitude toward the Jewish question, which was thoroughly different from mine. Hitler wanted to punish the Jews because he held them responsible for unleashing the war and for the bombing of the German population. . . . I repudiate the mass killings . . . in the same way as they are repudiated by every decent German.
>
> Your Honors! Neither in my capacity as Gauleiter nor as political author have I committed a crime, and I therefore look forward to your judgment with a good conscience.
>
> I have no request to make for myself. I have one for the German people from whom I come. Your Honors, fate has given you the power to pronounce any judgment. Do not pronounce a judgment which would imprint the stamp of dishonor upon the forehead of an entire nation.

Julius Streicher, sentenced to hang at Nuremberg, reads his last statement to the court.

Julius Streicher in his cell at Nuremberg. Streicher remained defiant and unrepentant until his death.

against humanity and pronounced sentence on him: "Death by hanging!"[58] ("*Tod durch den Strang!*")

On October 16, 1946, at the foot of the temporary gallows in the Nuremberg prison gymnasium, a defiant Streicher refused to give his name and instead shouted, "Heil Hitler!" He mounted the scaffold and yelled, "*Purim Fest*, 1946"—a reference to the celebration commemorating the deliverance of Persian Jews, when an advocate for their destruction was hanged in their stead. Turning to the hangman, he snarled, "Someday, the Bolsheviks will hang you!"[59] As the hangman slipped the hood over his head, Streicher said, "I am now by God my father! Adele my dear wife."[60] A moment later he disappeared through the trapdoor.

Reinhard Heydrich: God of Death

*G*listening sunlight and clear skies favored the morning of May 27, 1942. *Jan Kubiš and Josef Gabčík, two Free Czech agents trained in England, left the flat of schoolteacher Josef Orgoun, outside Prague, for a prearranged destination.*

Each man carried a battered briefcase. One briefcase contained a disassembled Sten gun; the other, two fused bombs of special design. The pair proceeded by tram to the Prague suburb of Zizkov, where they mounted waiting bicycles. With briefcases strapped to the handlebars, they peddled on their way to a covert rendezvous with Josef Valčík, a third Czech agent.

Shortly before 9:00 A.M., Kubiš and Gabčík arrived at a sloping street named V Holesovice, in the Liben district of the Czech capital. Valčík was already there.

Their rendezvous had been chosen carefully. It was the road traveled daily by Deputy Reich Protector Reinhard Heydrich, from Jungfern-Breschau, his country estate twenty minutes outside the city, to his office in the Hradcany Castle. The street led around a hairpin turn and down to the Traja Bridge over the Vltava River. All vehicles traversing the road had to slow down to negotiate the sharp turn.

The trio conferred briefly. Valčík then climbed to a vantage point at the top of the grade, carrying a mirror in his pocket for signaling. Kubiš and Gabčík positioned themselves

at the turn on either side of the street. Kubiš checked the contents of his briefcase. Gabčík assembled his Sten gun.

Their mission—Operation Anthropoid—had been conceived in London in October 1941 by the Czech government-in-exile. The three agents were now in place to carry out its final phase. But first they endured more than an hour of apprehensive waiting.

At 10:32 A.M. Valčík flashed his mirror, signaling that he had sighted their target. Moments later a green open-top Mercedes touring car, with an SS flag attached to one fender and a Reich Protector pennant to the other, started down the hill toward Kubiš and Gabčík.

When the Mercedes slowed for the hairpin curve, Gabčík leveled his Sten gun and took aim. Kubiš shouted "Now!"[61] and Gabčík squeezed the trigger. To the horror of both men, the gun misfired. Gabčík then stood helplessly exposed. Heydrich spotted him and reached for his pistol. But a passing tram temporarily shielded his would-be assassin.

In desperation, Kubiš tossed one of his bombs toward the Mercedes, but it fell short. It exploded, shattering the windows of the tram and disabling Heydrich's vehicle in an enormous flash of light and a cloud of black smoke. When a shower of flying metal and glass settled and the smoke cleared, Reinhard Heydrich and his driver, Oberscharführer (technical sergeant) Klein, leaped from the wrecked touring car with pistols drawn and started after their attackers. . . .

Himmler's Henchman

In the view of many who inquire into history, Reinhard Heydrich was the cruelest Nazi of them all, feared more by his contemporaries than either Heinrich Himmler or Adolf Hitler himself. German-born author and historian John Weitz, who worked for the American Office of Strategic Services (OSS) during World War II, aptly described Heydrich as "the coldest, most brutal man in the cold and brutal SS."[62]

The ruthlessly ambitious and duplicitous Heydrich even looked evil. Walter Schellenberg, Heydrich's chief of espionage and foreign counterintelligence, once described his mentor's sinister appearance this way:

> He was a tall, impressive figure with a broad, unusually high forehead, small restless eyes as crafty as an animal's and of uncanny power, and a wide full-lipped mouth. His hands were slender and rather too long—they made one think of the legs of a spider. His splendid figure was marred by the breadth of his hips, a disturbingly feminine effect which made him appear even more sinister. His voice was much too high for so large a man and his speech was nervous and staccato.[63]

Wilhelm Höttl, who served under Schellenberg, saw Heydrich as a man without a moral agenda:

> Truth and goodness had no intrinsic meaning for him; they were instruments to be used for the gaining of more and more power. . . . Politics too were . . .

merely stepping stones for the seizing and holding of power. To debate whether any action was of itself right appeared so stupid to him that it was certainly a question he never asked himself.[64]

Heydrich, Höttl concluded, possessed "a cruel, brave and cold intelligence [that manifested itself in] an unbroken chain of murders."[65]

Much has been written about Reinhard Heydrich, but the diligent researcher will find it difficult to uncover more than a line

Reinhard Heydrich was described as "the coldest, most brutal man in the cold and brutal SS."

or two about him that does not reek of evil. The Butcher of Prague, the Hangman, the Blond Beast—all names often applied to Heydrich—are hardly suggestive of tender mercies resident in his personality. Yet, it was his very capacity for evil that speeded his phenomenal rise in the ranks of the SS, on his way to becoming Himmler's indispensable henchman.

Sowing the Seeds of Fear

Reinhard Tristan Eugen Heydrich was born in Halle, a rural town in Prussian Saxony, on March 7, 1904. The son of a prominent Dresden music teacher, he grew up with a love of classical music and a talent for the violin, which he cultivated throughout his lifetime. In his later years he could still bow a heart-stirring composition with great feeling and technical excellence, often weeping freely as he played. But it was his association at age eighteen with Halle's Civil Defense Corps, a *Freikorps* formed to oppose local Communists, that caused him to consider a military calling.

Heydrich entered the German navy (Reichsmarine) on March 30, 1922, attaining the sea-service rank of first lieutenant (*Oberleutnant-zur-See*) before his naval career foundered in 1931. Following a scandal involving the daughter of a shipyard director, he was court-martialed and forced to resign for "conduct unworthy of an officer."[66]

In July of that same year, he joined the Nazi Party and then the SS. The tall, trim, blond, blue-eyed Heydrich soon attracted the attention of Himmler, who saw in Heydrich all the qualities of the Nordic-Aryan bloodline the *Reichsführer-SS* wanted so much to perpetuate in a new master race of Germans. Heydrich made SS major (*SS-Sturmbannführer*) on Christmas Day 1931—in the month he married Lina von Osten—and thereafter continued his amazingly rapid ascent to high office.

Himmler appointed Heydrich SS colonel (*SS-Standartenführer*) and chief of SS security (which later evolved into the SD) in July 1932, then SS major general (*SS-Brigadeführer*) eight months later. Serving as Himmler's right-hand man, Heydrich

Reinhard Heydrich (right) in Vienna in 1938. Heydrich's Aryan looks made him a favorite of Himmler (left).

helped his boss gain control, first of the Munich police, then of the Bavarian police, and finally of all the police in Germany. In 1934 Heydrich played a key role in helping to orchestrate and implement Himmler's blood purge of rival Nazi leaders on the night of June 29–30—the Night of the Long Knives.

Gregor Strasser, leader of the Nazi Party's liberal element, was among those arrested by Gestapo agents during the purge. Taken to a prison cell and shot in the back of the head by an SS man, Strasser bled profusely but did not die immediately. Hans Gisevius, the German vice-consul in Zurich during World War II who was involved in several conspiracies against Hitler, later wrote:

> A prisoner in the adjoining cell heard him thrashing about on the cot for nearly an hour. No one paid any attention to him. At last the prisoner heard loud footsteps in the corridor and orders being shouted. The guards clicked their heels. And the prisoner recognized Heydrich's voice saying, "Isn't he dead yet? Let the swine bleed to death." [67]

"An able technician of power, ruthless, cold and calculating, without any compunction in carrying out the most inhuman measures, Heydrich made himself indispensable to the masters of the Third Reich," according to Robert S. Wistrich. The eminent historian of Nazi Germany goes on to describe how Heydrich operated:

> As head of SIPO [Sicherheitspolizei], the unified, centralized, militarized and Nazified security police (including political and criminal police), Heydrich reacted with pitiless harshness in dealing with "enemies of the State." His cynicism and contempt for human beings led him to exploit the basest instincts—sadism, envy, intolerance—in weaving his gigantic spider web of police surveillance in the Third Reich. He filed extensive dossiers not only on enemies of the Party but also on his rivals and colleagues, using the police apparatus to set his opponents at each other's throats. "Scientific" studies of the *modus operandi* [method of procedure] of potential enemies of the State like Marxists, Jews, Freemasons, Liberal Republicans, [and] religious and cultural groups went hand and hand with arrests, torture and murder of those who stood in the way of the totalitarian police apparatus. [68]

Through such actions and procedures—in all of which he exhibited the ruthlessness and arrogance that became his trademarks—Heydrich earned the respect of Himmler and Hitler, and sowed the seeds of fear across Germany.

Master of Treachery and Deceit

On November 7, 1938, Herschel Grynszpan, a young Polish student in Paris, assassinated Ernst vom Rath, a minor official at the German embassy. The young man stated that the slaying was in response to the maltreatment of his parents by the Nazis.

Heydrich retaliated by ordering the destruction of all Jewish places of worship in Germany and Austria. Such an attack against the Jews had been long prepared; vom Rath's assassination merely provided the Germans with an excuse to launch the attack. (Suggestions stemming from some sources that Heydrich may have had a hand in arranging vom Rath's slaying have gone unsubstantiated.)

On the night of November 9–10, 1938, bands of Nazis roamed the streets of Germany, unhindered by the police, systematically destroying Jewish shops, offices, and synagogues. Streets littered with a huge amount of shattered glass from storefront windows gave name to the night of pillaging, thereafter known as *Kristallnacht* (literally, crystal night), or the Night of Broken Glass.

An SD report for the Nazi leadership summarized the night's activities like this:

The action manifested itself in general in the destruction or burning down of synagogues and the demolition of almost all Jewish businesses, which were thereby forced to sell up. In part the homes of Jews were affected in the action. . . . In resisting a number of Jews were killed or wounded.[69]

Of the SD report, historian and author Peter Padfield writes:

The report did not detail the exact extent of the damage or the number of deaths but an idea of scale can be gleaned from Heydrich's report to the ministerial meeting on the 12th: 7500

The ruins of a synagogue sanctuary after its destruction during Kristallnacht. *Heydrich ordered the destruction of all Jewish places of worship in Germany and Austria in retaliation for the death of German official Ernst vom Rath.*

businesses destroyed, 267 synagogues burned or damaged, 177 of them totally destroyed. Some ninety-one Jews were killed, but this figure was soon overtaken by the number beaten or otherwise done to death by the Totenkopf [death's head] guards in the concentration camps—according to some accounts more than a thousand.

The report merely stated that "in order to strengthen the compulsion to emigrate," 25,000 male Jews had been taken to concentration camps "for the moment temporarily." [Prior to World War II, the Nazis encouraged Jews to emigrate as an early means of dealing with the so-called Jewish problem.] The report concluded: "In summary it can be stated that Jewry—so far as German nationals and stateless persons are concerned—has finally been excluded from all areas of the German community so that only emigration remains to the Jews to safeguard their existence."[70]

In August 1939 Hitler needed an excuse to invade Poland. He no doubt recalled the success of Heydrich's staged rampage against the Jews on *Kristallnacht*. Hitler called on the cunning SD leader to arrange another staged event. Historian John Weitz provides a brief description of the event—code named Operation Tannenberg—in the following extract:

An SS captain, Alfred Naujocks, was ordered by Heydrich to "capture" a German radio station on the Polish border at Gleiwitz, using SS men in stolen Polish uniforms. The radio station was then to broadcast a Polish-language appeal. The men were to dress dead concentration camp inmates in Polish uniforms (the

By Fire and Sword

On November 11, 1938, following a glut of adverse world opinion in the aftermath of *Kristallnacht*, Hitler issued a mandate to Hermann Göring to resolve the Jewish question "one way or another." "Göring summoned a large number of officials from various agencies to a meeting at the Air Ministry in Berlin on November 12," writes Richard Breitman in *Architect of Genocide: Himmler and the Final Solution*:

Göring dominated much of the meeting on November 12, but Heydrich got in some good shots toward the end. He warned that the measures they were considering—to fine, identify, and restrict the Jews within Germany—would prove inadequate; the only solution was to get rid of them.

Breitman conveys Heydrich's views with an article that appeared in *Das Schwarze Korps* [*Black Corps*], the official weekly of the SS.

The Jews must be driven from our residential districts and segregated where they will be among themselves, having as little contact with Germans as possible. . . . Confined to themselves, these parasites will be . . . reduced to poverty. . . . Let no one fancy, however, that we shall then stand idly by, merely watching the process. . . . These hundreds of thousands of impoverished Jews [would create] a breeding ground for Bolshevism and a collection of the politically criminal subhuman elements. . . . In such a situation we would be faced with the hard necessity of exterminating the Jewish underworld. . . . The result would be the actual and final end of Jewry in Germany, its absolute annihilation.

Gestapo called the cadavers "canned goods") and leave them around the radio station's grounds as if they had been killed by German border police during the skirmish. The attack was made, and Naujocks was the moment's SS hero. The German police reported the attack and said that some Polish attackers were shot by German frontier guards. The *Völkische Beobachter* [*Racial Observer*; the official newspaper of the Nazi Party] bellowed POLISH PARTISANS CROSS GERMAN BORDER.[71]

"The closer you were to Heydrich," Naujocks said much later, "the more you learned to fear him."[72] And rightly so, for Heydrich had once again proved himself a master of treachery and deceit.

"The Worst of Sadists"

Warsaw, Poland's capital, fell to Hitler's legions on September 27, 1939. On that same day Himmler created the Reich Central Security Office (RSHA) and placed Heydrich at its head. The new office combined the secret state police (Gestapo), the

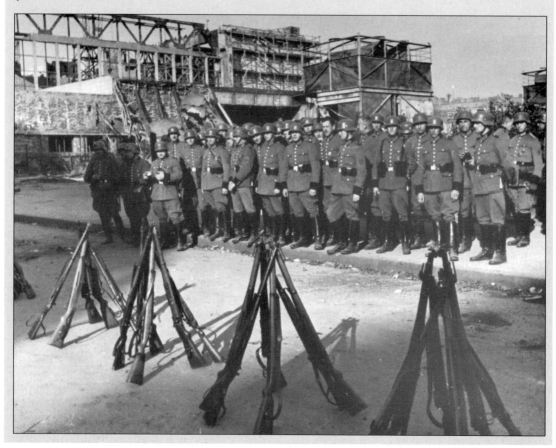

German troops in Warsaw in 1939. Heydrich staged a mock battle, saying that the Germans were attacked by the Poles as an excuse to enter Poland.

criminal police (*Kriminalpolizei*, or KRIPO), and the Nazi Party security service (SD) under a single organizational umbrella. It also served as the central office of the Reich Interior Ministry. Heydrich took on the title of chief of the security police and security service (*Chef der Sicherheitspolizei und des SD*, or CSSD). The creation of the RSHA represented no major change in leadership, however, as Heydrich had earlier been appointed head of the three individual agencies now consolidated as one.

Seven departments were set up within the RSHA: personnel; organization, administration, and law; SD domestic intelligence; political police (Gestapo); criminal police (KRIPO); SD foreign intelligence; and ideological research and evaluation. But most important among RSHA's activities were intelligence gathering at home and abroad; policing, including the suppression of the Nazis' political enemies, both inside Germany and in Nazi-occupied lands; and the elimination of Jews and others deemed racially inferior by the Nazis. The newly appointed head of RSHA had already initiated measures to achieve the latter in Poland:

German soldiers round up prisoners after entering Poland.

> Heydrich's Einsatzkommandos [literally, killer units; small detachments of *Einsatzgruppen*] were following the advancing armies, rounding up Jews, aristocrats, priests and the professional classes in every community they entered. In some cases they took their victims to "reception centers" for execution, in some cases simply stood them against a wall and shot them or hung them in rows from long beams in the market place; on other occasions they made deadly sport, chasing Jews through the streets or into synagogues, hurling grenades in after them, setting fire to buildings and burning them alive.[73]

In parallel with the mass killings, Heydrich initiated ghettoization. The ghettos, purported as permanent places of settlement by the murderous Nazis, were really roundup centers to facilitate the wholesale slaughter of Jews later. Heydrich then ordered the Jews to establish Jewish councils (*Judenräte*) in each ghetto community. "These councils were to carry out the instructions of the special SS task forces (*Einsatzgruppen*)," writes historian Klaus B. Fischer, "for instance compiling accurate lists of persons and their assets. In other words, the Jews were to organize their own destruction and pay for every penny of it—a scheme worthy of the worst of sadists."[74]

Poland proved to be only a training ground for the murderous activities of Heydrich's *Einsatzgruppen*, only the forerunner of a far more vast killing campaign to follow. By establishing the Central Office for Jewish Emigration in January 1939—headed first by Gestapo chief Heinrich Müller and soon thereafter by Adolf Eichmann—Heydrich had already taken steps toward developing a new kind of social engineering.

Under Eichmann's direction, the new agency applied modern management techniques to the rounding up, robbing, and forced emigration of Jews from Austria. But as a result of rapid German military successes in western Europe and the severance of more and more emigration routes, forced emigration could not keep pace with the increasingly large numbers of Jews that fell under the pall of German dominance. The Jewish "problem" was clearly escalating.

It remains unclear as to when the Nazis' policy of genocide received final approval. But with Germany's invasion of the Soviet

Hungry residents gather in the marketplace of the Warsaw ghetto in 1940. The Nazis used the money they had robbed from the Jews to pay for the construction of the ghetto.

"A Bitter Stroke of Irony"

Although Hitler ordered the Wehrmacht (German army) not to interfere with *Einsatzgruppen* operations, Reinhard Heydrich's killer units sometimes provoked harsh criticism from the officers and men of German regular army units. In *Hitler's Diplomat: The Life and Times of Joachim von Ribbentrop*, historian John Weitz writes of the futile protests of one high-ranking critic:

> The special SS men with the SD diamond patch on their sleeves began to commit such acts of brutality and bestiality that word soon reached the top echelons of the Army.
>
> Then, to the deep shock of the SD and its chief, Reinhard Heydrich, Colonel General Johannes Blaskowitz, the [German] Army commander in Poland, interfered. He would not permit the Army to be complacent witnesses and passive collaborators in things that the general considered abominable. He had many reports of shameful acts. He collected these and sent a written protest about the mass murders and other SD debauches to the Army chief of staff.
>
> General Blaskowitz said it affected Army morale to witness this SD swinishness. The memorandum was read by Adolf Hitler on November 18, 1939. He was furious with the general, but Blaskowitz was undeterred. The field generals under his command continued to report SD atrocities all over Poland. Poles were shot arbitrarily. Jews were beaten, humiliated, and killed, men, women, children, and babies, sometimes in their synagogues. There was rape and looting.
>
> Blaskowitz's next memorandum stated that "the attitude of the troops toward SD and police alternates between abhorrence and hatred. Every soldier feels disgusted by these crimes committed in Poland by nationals of the Reich and representatives of our state." Several generals at Hitler's headquarters joined Blaskowitz in expressing revulsion. Army officers at Blaskowitz's headquarters would no longer shake hands with SS officers. Himmler finally had to order an investigation, but it was a sham. Blaskowitz was relieved of his command in 1940 by Adolf Hitler and never promoted, although as a talented general he was given a command in the western campaign. In a bitter stroke of irony, he was arrested by the Allies at the end of the war and charged with war crimes. It was too much for him to bear. He committed suicide in a Nürnberg [Nuremberg] prison in February 1948.

Fellow prisoners suspected that Blaskowitz had been assassinated by SS men but their suspicions have never been confirmed.

Union on June 22, 1941—Operation Barbarossa—the need for a more radical approach to the "Jewish question" became apparent to the Nazi leadership. On July 31, 1941, six weeks after the German invasion of the Soviet Union, Reich Marshal Hermann Göring issued the following directive to Reinhard Heydrich:

> In completion of the task which was entrusted to you in the Edict dated January 24, 1939, of solving the Jewish

question by means of emigration or evacuation in the most convenient way possible, given the present conditions, I herewith charge you with making all necessary preparations with regard to organizational, practical, and financial aspects for an overall solution [*Gesamtlösung*] of the Jewish question in the German sphere of influence in Europe. Insofar as competencies of other central organizations are affected, these are to be involved. I further charge you with submitting to me promptly an overall plan of the preliminary organizational, practical, and financial measures for the execution of the intended final solution [*Endlösung*] of the Jewish question.[75]

Under Heydrich's direction, construction of death camps began in December, designed specifically for the mass destruction of the Jews, in an undertaking later named Operation (*Aktion*) Reinhard in his honor. At the same time, newly formed units of *Einsatzgruppen* were following the advancing German armies into the Soviet Union, slaughtering every Jew, Gypsy, Slav, and local Soviet government official they could find.

"Free of All Guilt"

On September 27, 1941, Hitler appointed Heydrich deputy reich protector for Bohemia and Moravia. Heydrich began his new duties by proclaiming a state of emergency in Prague. He immediately executed everyone already arrested for treasonable acts, killing some four hundred prisoners during the state of emergency. And he arrested over five thousand suspected members of resistance groups by November. But the so-called Butcher of Prague had been charged with an even greater responsibility.

On January 20, 1942, Heydrich chaired a meeting in the Berlin suburb of Grossen-Wannsee (the infamous Wannsee Conference). The fourteen others in attendance included Gestapo chief Heinrich Müller and Jewish affairs expert Adolf Eichmann. Heydrich informed them that he had been vested with full power to carry out "the final solution to the Jewish question."

Heydrich told them that Hitler had sanctioned the evacuation of all Jews to the east as a "solution possibility."[76] "The Jews will be conscripted for labor," he continued, "and undoubtedly a large number of them will drop out through natural wastage."[77] Those Jews hardy enough to survive work assignments would be "treated accordingly,"[78] which clearly implied that they would be killed. Thus work became just another means for killing Jews. (That "work" and "death" meant the same thing for Jews was confirmed by Himmler during a meeting in October 1942. After temporarily assigning the Jews in the Warsaw and Lublin regions to a "few large concentration camp factories," he concluded, "Of course, there too, the Jews shall someday disappear in accordance with the Führer's wishes."[79])

Adolf Eichmann recorded the minutes of the meeting that set in motion plans for implementing the Final Solution and sealed the fate of several million Jews. After the conference, he joined Heydrich and Gestapo chief Müller to unwind, drinking and singing songs, sitting "cozily around a fireplace." Eichmann continued, "After a while we climbed onto the table and traipsed round and round—on the chairs and on the table again." He later testified, "At that moment I sensed a kind of Pontius Pilate feeling, for I was free of all guilt. . . . Who was I to judge? Who was I to have my own thoughts in this matter?"[80] After all, the three of them were only carrying out the orders of their exalted führer.

Dancing to the Tune

Satisfied that the details for implementing the Final Solution had been worked out and would shortly turn into reality, Heydrich returned to Prague, where he continued "the policy of the whip and the sugar."[81] He accelerated his repressive measures and ordered mass executions, while simultaneously trying to win approval from workers and peasants by improving working and social conditions.

By then Heydrich saw himself as *Reichsführer-SS* Himmler's replacement and, beyond that, the logical successor to the führer himself. Many of his contemporaries agreed with his logic, but out of fear rather than respect. He frightened everyone, including Himmler and probably even Hitler. Ironi-cally, the very fear that speeded his rise to power and high office ultimately led to his own destruction.

After the explosion, an off-duty Czech policeman commandeered a small truck carrying a load of furniture polish. The policeman helped the badly—but not mortally—wounded Heydrich aboard the truck. The truck sped off to a nearby Bulkova hospital, arriving just after 11:00 A.M. A young Czech doctor, Vladimír Šnadjr, cleansed Heydrich's wounds and administered emergency treatment.

Himmler learned of the attack on Heydrich that afternoon. He dispatched his personal physician, Professor Karl Gebhardt, the surgeon general of the SS, to take over Heydrich's care from the Czech doctors. Heydrich fought hard for his life and appeared on June 3 to be recovering. But he succumbed suddenly to blood poisoning and died on June 4, 1942.

Reinhard Heydrich (far left) believed he would eventually replace Himmler (second from left), then Hitler. His plans were foiled when he died of blood poisoning after an assassination attack in 1942.

Operation Anthropoid ended successfully with a brief entry in the Bulkova hospital's register, listing the cause of death next to the name of Reinhard Tristan Eugen Heydrich: "Wound infection."[82]

Shortly before Heydrich died, Himmler had visited him in the hospital. The *Reichsführer-SS* later told Lina Heydrich only that her husband had quoted some lines from one of his father's operas: "Yes, the world is but a barrel organ, which our Lord God turns himself, and each must dance to the tune, exactly as it stands on the drum."[83] For Heydrich, the music lover, the tune had ended, never to be danced to again.

Terror from the Grave

Following Heydrich's assassination, the Germans conducted a great manhunt, wantonly slaughtering Czechs in reprisal for his death. Author and journalist Alan Levy summarizes the German savagery:

> His assassins took sanctuary in the crypt of the Orthodox Church of Sts Cyril and Methodius in Prague, where they shot themselves to death when the Gestapo closed in. In retaliation, the church's bishop, two ministers, the chaplain, and the chairman of its parish council, as well as more than a hundred Czechs accused of aiding the assassins and another 1357 accused of "approving of the assassination" were massacred by the SS. Less than a week after Heydrich died, the Czech village of Lidice was destroyed in his memory.[84]

In Heydrich's honor, SS leaders later assigned the code name Operation Reinhard to their systematic destruction of Jews in Nazi-occupied Europe. From March 1942 to December 1943, Operation Reinhard murderers slaughtered 2,284,000 Jews. "In death as in life," writes historian Wistrich, "Heydrich's name seemed inextricably linked with terror and intimidation for its own sake."[85] And so it must have seemed to Carl Jacob Burckhardt, onetime president of the International Red Cross, who so fittingly labeled Heydrich "a young evil god of death."[86]

CHAPTER 4

Adolf Eichmann: Grand Inquisitor

"The worst story I can ever tell you about Adolf Eichmann," said famed Nazi-hunter Simon Wiesenthal to author Alan Levy, "took place during the time he was in Budapest." Wiesenthal continued:

> In the fall of 1944, a group of high-level SS officers were sitting in the SS casino there. And one of them asked Eichmann how many people had been exterminated already.
>
> Eichmann said: "Over five million."
>
> Well, because he was among comrades and they all knew it was only a matter of months before they would lose the war, one of them asked whether he was worried about what would happen to him.
>
> Eichmann gave a very astute answer that shows he knew how the world worked: "A hundred dead people is a catastrophe," he said. "Six million dead is a statistic."[87]

As chief of the Gestapo's Jewish Office (Section IV B4) of the RSHA, SS lieutenant colonel (*SS-Obersturmbannführer*) Adolf Eichmann represented the epitome of desk murderers. Responsible for rounding up and deporting between five and six million Jews and others to their deaths in Nazi extermination centers, few if any ordinary Germans worked harder than Eichmann to wipe out the Jews of Europe.

As chief of the Jewish Office of the RSHA, Adolf Eichmann was responsible for deporting between five and six million Jews.

The Self-Taught Expert

Karl Adolf Eichmann's contempt for Jews began early. Born in Solingen, Germany, on March 19, 1906, he grew up in Linz, Austria, as did the führer, whom he would serve so faithfully as an adult. In his youth, because of his own Jewish-like appearance, friends called him *"der kleine Jude"* [88] ("the little Jew"). Later, while working as a traveling salesman for an oil company, he came to loathe the Jews he met in Vienna. His frequent attendance at Nazi meetings did little to allay his anti-Semitic aversions.

In 1927 Eichmann joined the youth section of the Austro-German Veterans' Organization. Then, encouraged by Ernst Kaltenbrunner, who would later replace Reinhard Heydrich as chief of the RSHA, Eichmann joined the Nazi Party in 1932.

Eichmann lost his job in the spring of 1933. In July, with the Nazi Party and its affiliates suspended in Austria because of Hitler's rise to power, he crossed the border into Bavaria and joined the newly forming Austrian legion-in-exile. He underwent fourteen months of training but soon wearied of military routine. "The humdrum of military service, that was something I couldn't stand, day after day always the same thing, over and over again the same." [89] When he learned of openings in the security service (*Sicherheitsdienst*, or SD) of Heinrich Himmler's SS, Eichmann applied at once and was accepted into the SD as a filing clerk.

He was first posted to the "Freemasons" section and later transferred to "Jews"—SD Office II 112—typing data on suspects under Nazi surveillance. Mostly on his own initiative, Eichmann began studying all the material he could find on both Freemasons and Jews. He soon convinced himself that the two groups were engaged in an international conspiracy to rule the world. He went on to become a self-taught expert in Jewish affairs.

Eichmann's bureaucratic talents and knowledge of Jews caught the attention of *Reichsführer-SS* Heinrich Himmler. Rupert Butler, chronicler of the Gestapo, writes:

> It was scarcely surprising that so assiduous a student of racial matters—moreover one who was as colorless as he was pedantic and punctilious—should receive the approval of Himmler. Eichmann extended his researches to the appropriate SD offices, working in conjunction with Gestapo Department IIB which had the task of carrying out actual surveillance. When Himmler created a Scientific Museum of Jewish Affairs as an agency of the SD, he appointed the enthusiastic Eichmann to head the project. Whenever he could, Eichmann attended Jewish gatherings, visited the Jewish quarters of many towns and cities, making copious notes and setting up systematic files. With growing confidence, he began to see himself, not simply as an archivist, but as an intelligence agent. [90]

In late 1937 Eichmann visited Palestine to explore possibilities of emigrating Jews from Nazi Germany to Palestine, but the British ordered him out of the country. Upon returning to Germany, he was commissioned a second lieutenant (*SS-Untersturmführer*) and cited for his "comprehensive knowledge of the methods of organization and ideology of the opponent, Jewry." [91]

Nothing More to Say

Eichmann's first big opportunity came after the *Anschluss* (Union), the German takeover of Austria. In August 1938 he was named to

German police march through the town of Imst during the 1938 invasion of Austria. After the invasion, Eichmann was appointed to head the SS Office for Jewish Emigration in Vienna.

head the SS Office for Jewish Emigration in Vienna—the sole Nazi agency authorized to issue exit permits for Jews, first from Austria, then Czechoslovakia, and later Germany itself. Charged with the "forced emigration" of Jews in Austria, an early attempt by the Nazis to solve the "Jewish problem," Eichmann excelled at his first important assignment. Historian Robert Edwin Herzstein recounts Eichmann's "stunning success" this way:

> He "cleansed" Austria of 45,000 Jews in the same eight-month period that saw

only 19,000 Jews evicted from Germany. In 18 months, he reduced Austria's Jewish population by about one half, to 150,000 people. What is more, he showed a tidy profit. His tactic, as Heydrich explained it, was the soul of simplicity: "Through the Jewish community, we extracted a certain amount of money from rich Jews who wanted to emigrate."[92]

Eichmann's successes in Austria brought him prominence and rapid advancement. Transferred first to Prague and then to Berlin, as head of the Reich Center for Jewish

"A Family Legend"

In *Eichmann in Jerusalem: A Report on the Banality of Evil*, her masterwork on the Eichmann trial, Hannah Arendt describes how he perceived himself as a benefactor of the Jews:

> During the cross-examination, he told the presiding judge that in Vienna he "regarded the Jews as opponents with respect to whom a mutually acceptable, a mutually fair solution had to be found. . . . That solution I envisaged as putting firm soil under their feet so that they would have a place of their own, soil of their own. . . . This was the true reason they had all "pulled together," the reason their work had been "based upon mutuality." It was in the interest of the Jews, though perhaps not all Jews understood this, to get out of the country; "one had to help them, one had to help these functionaries to act, and that's what I did." If the Jewish functionaries were "idealists," that is, Zionists [advocates of a Jewish state], he respected them, "treated them as equals," listened to all their "requests and complaints and applications for support," kept his "promises" as far as he could—"People are inclined to forget that now." Who but he, Eichmann, had saved hundreds of thousands of Jews? What but his great zeal and gifts of organization had enabled them to escape in time? True, he could not foresee at the time the coming of the Final Solution, but he had saved them, that was a "fact."

Parenthetically, Arendt adds: "In an interview given in this country [the United States] during the trial, Eichmann's son told the same story to American reporters. It must have been a family legend."

Emigration, he began deporting Jews to Poland. In December 1939 he was transferred again, this time as chief of the Gestapo's Section IV B4 dealing with Jewish affairs and evacuation. Herzstein continues:

> In recognition of his excellent performance in Austria, Eichmann was prepped for greater things with a series of broadening assignments, some for Gestapo chief Heinrich Müller, some for Heydrich himself. In 1941 and 1942, for example, Eichmann helped to organize the Theresienstadt ghetto north of Prague to accommodate prominent Jews whose disappearance would prompt embarrassing questions. This was part of an interim program of concentrating and isolating all Jews in convenient ghettos and labor camps. In June 1941, Eichmann, now a major [*SS-Sturmbannführer*], learned the reason for the program.[93]

Reinhard Heydrich, now chief of the Reich Central Security Office (RSHA), which incorporated the Gestapo, the criminal police, and the SD, summoned Eichmann to his Berlin office. Heydrich began his session with Eichmann with "a little speech about emigration," then said, "The Führer has ordered the extermination of the Jews."[94]

Eichmann claimed years later that he was stunned by Heydrich's revelation. "In the first moment, I was unable to grasp the significance of what he said, because he was so careful in choosing his words, and then I understood, and didn't say anything, because there was nothing to say any more."[95]

Bühler's Suggestion

For the duration of the war, Eichmann's Section IV B4 became the headquarters for implementing the Final Solution. (Under the

RSHA, Section IV was the Gestapo, headed by Heinrich Müller; subsection B handled sects and churches; and there were four branches: (1) Catholics, (2) Protestants, (3) Freemasons, and (4) Jews.) In the summer of 1941, Eichmann's section began developing the plans and apparatus for the destruction of European Jewry: creating death camps, developing gassing techniques for mass murder, and putting together a conveyance system for transporting the Jews to their final destinations. Eichmann was promoted to lieutenant colonel (*SS-Obersturmbannführer*) in November, his last promotion. It was a modest rank for someone who held the power of life or death over several million people, but apparently a rank indicative of what the Nazis felt his job was worth.

In January 1942 Eichmann attended the Wannsee Conference convened by his superior, RSHA chief Reinhard Heydrich, who now formally assigned him full responsibility for collecting and delivering Europe's Jews to their extinction. Eichmann, the lowest-ranking person present, kept the minutes of the meeting, which took less than an hour and a half, to plot the fate of eleven million Jews and actually murder more than six million of them.

The purpose of the meeting was to formally adopt the Final Solution—that is, the contemplated annihilation of the Jews—to review plans and preparations for its implementation already in process, and to suggest ways and means to facilitate and improve future operations. The meeting also served to underline anew Heydrich's authority and to consolidate Eichmann's position.

Following the formal announcement and discussion of the Final Solution, Dr. Josef Bühler, the highest official attending from occupied Poland, said, "I have only one favor to ask—that the Jewish problem in my area be solved as quickly as possible."

Adolf Eichmann was a pivotal person in the implementation of the Final Solution. His duties included creating death camps, developing gassing techniques, and developing a way to transport the Jews to the camps.

Years later, an Israeli interrogator asked Eichmann, "What is Bühler suggesting?"

Eichmann replied, "He is suggesting that they should be killed."[96]

No Tolerance for Suffering

Following the Wannsee meeting, Eichmann visited Rudolf Höss, camp commandant at the Auschwitz killing facility. Höss later recalled Eichmann's visit and his impressions of him:

I got to know him after I received the order from Himmler to exterminate the Jews. After that he came to Auschwitz to discuss all the details of the action to exterminate the Jews. Eichmann was a lively man in his thirties who always kept busy and was full of energy. He always came up with new plans and always looked for new ways, not just improvements. He was never at rest. He was possessed about the Jewish question and the Final Solution. Eichmann had to report continuously to Himmler directly and verbally about the preparations and the implementation of the individual roundups. Only Eichmann was in a position to furnish any information concerning the numbers. He could refer to almost anything from memory. His files consisted of a few pieces of notepaper with some unintelligible symbols. He constantly carried them around with him.[97]

Notwithstanding such crude tracking methods, Eichmann handled his new assignment with the same efficiency he had shown earlier in Austria, Prague, and Berlin. "In this task," observes Robert S. Wistrich, "Eichmann proved to be a model of bureaucratic industriousness and icy determination even though he had never been a fanatical antisemite and always claimed that 'personally' he had nothing against Jews."[98]

Over the next few months, Eichmann traveled about Poland and Russia to learn firsthand about the massive killing operations. On one occasion, Gestapo chief Heinrich Müller sent him to Minsk, in Belorussia, to witness the shooting of some Jews and to report on the details of how it was done. Eichmann later recalled arriving late at the execution site:

They had already started, so I could only see the finish. Although I was wearing a leather coat that reached almost to my ankles, it was very cold. I watched the last group of Jews undress, down to their shirts. They walked the last 100 or 200 yards—they were not driven—then they jumped into the pit. Then the men of the [killing] squad banged away into the pit with their rifles and machine pistols. I saw a woman hold a child of a year or two, pleading. Then the child was hit. I was so close that later I found bits of brains splattered on my long leather coat. My chauffeur helped me remove them.[99]

On a visit to Lodz, in central Poland, Eichmann became so distressed watching the gassing of a thousand Jews in sealed buses that he forgot to time the event. He later explained his loss of composure to a disapproving Müller, saying, "I simply cannot look at any suffering without trembling myself."[100]

Cyclon B

During another visit with Rudolf Höss at Auschwitz, which was soon to become the largest and most efficient death camp, Eichmann revealed secret plans for rounding up Jews in the individual European countries and transporting them to Auschwitz for extermination. Höss recalled in his memoirs that Eichmann had been extremely helpful:

We further discussed how the mass annihilation was to be carried out. Only gas was suitable since killing by shooting the huge numbers expected would be absolutely impossible and would put a tremendous strain on the SS soldiers who would have to carry out the order as far as the women and children were concerned.

Eichmann told me about the killings by engine exhaust gas in the gas vans and how they had been used in the East up until now. But this method was not suitable in view of the expected mass transports to Auschwitz. We also discussed killing by carbon monoxide through the shower heads in the shower rooms, but this would create a problem because too many intricate installations would be needed. . . . [And] the production of such great quantities of gas for such large numbers of people would be a problem. We didn't reach any decision about this. Eichmann wanted to find a gas that was easy to produce and one that would require no special installations; he then would report back to me.

After that meeting, Höss started experimenting with Cyclon (also spelled Zyclon or Zyklon) B, a gas used for insect and rodent control. "During Eichmann's next visit," wrote Höss, "I told him about the use of Cyclon B and we decided to use it for the mass extermination operations."[101] The first attempt to kill people using Cyclon B at Auschwitz took place on September 3, 1941.

A Reason to Hang

Although one of the most powerful and feared of all the Nazi war criminals, Adolf Eichmann worked in the shadows and did not gain wide public recognition until late in the war. As related by Wistrich:

Containers of Cyclon B, seized from Auschwitz. Adolf Eichmann was responsible for the decision to use this commercial pesticide for mass exterminations.

Only in Budapest after March 1944 did the desk-murderer [Eichmann] become a public personality, working in the open and playing a leading role in the massacre of Hungarian Jewry. In August of 1944 the "Grand Inquisitor" of European Jewry could report to Himmler that approximately four million Jews had died in the death camps and another two million had been killed by mobile extermination units.[102]

Many years after the end of World War II, Simon Wiesenthal told Alan Levy that Eichmann had become so fanatical by the end of 1944 that "when even Himmler ordered Eichmann to stop the killing in Hungary, he no longer understood the word 'Stop!' any more."[103]

Historian Rupert Butler called Eichmann the "assistant architect of the Final Solution."[104] Certainly no one was more deserving of the title than Eichmann for having deported millions of Jews to their deaths. Yet knowledge of the depth and breadth of his crimes did not surface in the Western world until long after the end of the war. Though arrested by the Allies, Eichmann's name was still not widely known then, and he managed to escape from an internment camp in the American zone. Then, like many Nazis before and after him, Eichmann fled to South America.

In 1960, following a fifteen-year manhunt, Israeli agents abducted him in a Buenos Aires suburb and returned him to Israel to stand trial for his crimes. Eichmann pleaded not guilty on fifteen counts, but the Israeli court found to the contrary. Hannah Arendt paraphrased the conclusion of the court's judgment this way:

And just as you supported and carried out a policy of not wanting to share the earth with the Jewish people and the people of a number of other nations—as though you

The identification papers that Adolf Eichmann used after the war. After living for years in Argentina under the assumed name of Ricardo Klement, Eichmann was eventually abducted and brought to Israel for trial..

During the war crimes trial in Israel, Judge Landau reads Eichmann's sentence—to hang for the crimes he committed against the Jewish people and for crimes against humanity.

and your superiors had any right to determine who should and who should not inhabit the world—we find that no one, that is, no member of the human race, can be expected to want to share the earth with you. This is the reason, and the only reason, you must hang.[105]

And hang he did—for crimes against the Jewish people and crimes against humanity—in Israel's Ramleh prison on May 31, 1962. He had had fifteen years to prepare for his end. Hannah Arendt wrote that "Adolf Eichmann went to the gallows with great dignity."[106]

Rudolf Höss: Death Dealer

In the summer of 1941, Heinrich Himmler summoned SS captain (*SS-Hauptsturmführer*) Rudolf Höss to his Berlin headquarters. Höss was commandant of the concentration camp at Auschwitz. To Höss's mild surprise, he found Himmler alone in his office. Usually Himmler's adjutant sat in during such visits but not this time. The SS chief clearly intended that this meeting be held in strict confidentiality. Himmler greeted Höss and said:

> The Führer has ordered the Final Solution of the Jewish question. We the SS have to carry out this order. The existing extermination sites in the East [areas where mobile killing squads conducted mass murders; there were, as yet, no permanent extermination centers in the East] are not in a position to carry out these intended operations on a large scale. I have therefore chosen Auschwitz for this purpose. First of all, because of the advantageous transport facilities, and secondly, because it allows this area to be easily isolated and disguised. I had first thought of choosing a higher-ranking SS officer for this job so as to avoid any difficulties with someone who doesn't have the competence to deal with such a difficult assignment. You

now have to carry out this assignment. It is to remain between the two of us. It is a hard and difficult job which requires

Rudolf Höss during his testimony at the Nuremberg trials. Höss was the commandant of Auschwitz concentration camp. On the stand, he admitted ordering the deaths of 2.5 million people.

your complete commitment, regardless of the difficulties which might arise.[107]

With those words, Heinrich Himmler had consigned to death some 2.5 million existing or eventual inmates of Auschwitz by execution, mostly Jews, and another half million through slow starvation. In conclusion, Himmler warned:

> The Jews are the eternal enemies of the German people and must be exterminated. All the Jews within our reach must be annihilated during this war. If we do not succeed in destroying the biological foundation of Jewry now, then one day the Jews will destroy the German people.[108]

In his memoirs Höss made no mention of his response to Himmler's mandate, except to call it a "far-reaching order."[109]

"The Low Point"

If Himmler held any doubts as to whether he had picked the right man for the job, he need not have. Höss applied himself to his new assignment with energy and enthusiasm. Gerald Reitlinger, a noted historian of the SS and the Final Solution, writes:

> Within a few weeks, on 15 September, Höss conducted an experiment on invalid Russian prisoners of war in the sealed penal block of Auschwitz main camp. He used a commercial preparation, which was supplied to the camp as a disinfectant gas, the blue hydrogen-cyanide crystals, known as Zyclon B [also spelled Zyklon or Cyclon]. Höss was ordered to adopt this system permanently in March 1942, when a small gas chamber was installed in a converted

barn near the evacuated village of Birkenwald.[110]

Höss, as many others like him, considered himself a decent, loving family man, bound by duty to perform an unpleasant but essential task. He feared himself to be of a more sensitive nature than some of his SS colleagues and tried to hide his sensitivity with an icy exterior. He found the gassing of victims preferable to shooting them. He said later:

> I must admit that the gassing process had a calming effect on me. I always had a horror of the [earlier] shootings, thinking of the number of people, the women and children. I was relieved that we were spared these blood baths.[111]

By May 1944 the extermination process at Auschwitz reached peak efficiency, Höss reported later, routinely killing "something over 9000"[112] victims every twenty-four hours.

In 1945, while testifying at Nuremberg, commandant Höss explained the improvements he had made, enabling Auschwitz to surpass the horrid output of other death camps:

> We tried to fool the victims into believing that they were going through a delousing process. Of course, at times they realized our true intentions and we sometimes had riots and difficulties. Frequently women would hide their children under their clothes, but we found them and we sent the children to be exterminated. We were required to carry out these exterminations in secrecy, but the foul and nauseating stench from the continued burning of bodies

permeated the whole area and all the people living around Auschwitz knew what was going on.[113]

When Höss confessed to the killing of 2.5 million people, fellow defendant Hans Frank told prison psychologist G. M. Gilbert: "That was the low point of the entire trial . . . that is something that people will talk about for a thousand years."[114]

Call to the Camps

Rudolf Franz Höss was born in Baden-Baden, Germany, on November 25, 1900. As the son of a pious shopkeeper who once wanted him to become a priest, Rudolf grew up in an environment of total obedience. "It was emphatically pointed out again and again that I carry out the requests and orders of parents, teachers, priests, and all adults, even the servants," Höss recalled in his memoirs, "and that this principle be respectfully obeyed." Such strict early train-

A dead prisoner is pushed into an oven at Auschwitz. Höss oversaw such operations.

ing instilled in him a profound sense that all orders should "be performed exactly and conscientiously."[115]

In his future role as Heinrich Himmler's chief agent of death, Höss "respectfully" obeyed all of the *Reichsführer*'s orders to the letter, meticulously and without question. When Himmler "personally" notified him of plans to make Auschwitz "the largest human killing center in all of history,"[116] Höss did not blink an eye. Frequently touted as the most sinister of all Nazis, Höss followed a checkered path to prominence in the Nazi bureaucracy.

Before the age of fifteen, Höss served with the German army in Turkey. Wounded several times, he earned the Iron Cross (First and Second Classes) for bravery. At seventeen, he became the youngest noncommissioned officer in the German forces. After the war, he joined the Rossbach *Freikorps* (a paramilitary group of mercenaries comprising mostly ex-soldiers) and participated in battles in the Baltic region, the Ruhr, and Upper Silesia.

In 1923 Höss was arrested—along with Martin Bormann, who eventually became Hitler's chief adviser—for the political assassination of Walther Kadow, the alleged betrayer of Albert Leo Schlageter, a martyred Nazi hero. Höss and Bormann remained close friends in prison and both were released on a general amnesty in 1928. Bormann would later assist Höss in his Nazi career.

After his release from prison, Höss worked the land with the Artamans—an organization of young nationalists dedicated to the concept of settling on the soil—for the next six years.

Among the Artamans, he met and married "the woman I had dreamed of during the long years of my solitude."[117] A notable leader among the Artamans, who were devoted to the idea of *Blut und Boden* (Blood and Soil), was Heinrich Himmler.

Höss's career took off when Hitler assumed power in January 1933. In June 1934 Himmler invited Höss to join the active SS, on the promise of "quick promotion" and "all the financial advantages connected with it." As Höss would write years later:

> When Himmler made the call to join the SS, to enter the guard troop of a concentration camp, I had no thought at all about the concentration camps which were mentioned in the postscript. During the isolation of our farm life in Pomerania, we had hardly heard about concentration camps. The only thing I could see was the active military life of being a soldier again.[118]

It is worth mentioning that in Nazi Germany of 1934—whether isolated or not— few people, if any, did not know about the concentration camps. In any case, Höss joined the SS and was assigned to the Dachau concentration camp as a noncommissioned officer in the guard troop, where he began his apprenticeship in learning the skills of his profane profession.

Rudolf Höss arrived at Dachau with the rank of SS sergeant (*SS-Unterscharführer*) and underwent a kind of basic training. During instruction and lectures, he learned about the use of arms and about the inherently "dangerous nature of the ENEMIES OF THE STATE, as Inspector of the Concentration Camps [Theodor] Eicke called the prisoners behind the barbed wire."[119] (Dachau, twelve miles northwest of Munich,

was established in 1933 to incarcerate political prisoners exclusively; in 1937 its role was expanded to include asocials, habitual criminals, homosexuals, Jehovah's Witnesses, Jews, and others.) After six months, Höss was elevated to block overseer, responsible for 270 inmates, a position that he approached with some misgivings:

> With mixed feelings, I entered into my new area of responsibility, into a new world to which I would be chained for the next ten years. Yes, I had been a prisoner myself for six long years, and I knew about the life of a prisoner. I knew his habits, his good and bad sides, all his impulses and needs, but the concentration camp was new to me. I was to learn the tremendous difference between life in a jail or prison and life in a concentration camp. And I learned it from the ground up, often more thoroughly than I really liked.[120]

Höss later professed disagreement with Theodor Eicke's stringent and often brutal policies at Dachau. But he learned and executed them well because he "wanted to have the reputation of being hard" and "did not want to be thought of as a weak person."[121] To Höss, image was everything.

"A True Pioneer"

Höss was transferred to Sachsenhausen concentration camp, north of Berlin, on August 1, 1938, to serve as camp adjutant under SS colonel (*SS-Standartenführer*) Hermann Baranowski. Höss appraised his new camp commandant as "strict and hard" but with "a keen sense of justice and a fanatical sense of duty. He became my model of an old National Socialist and SS officer." Baranowski "also had moments in which his

"Too Much Compassion for the Prisoners"

In *Death Dealer: The Memoirs of the SS Kommandant at Auschwitz*, Rudolf Höss gained insight into what he categorized as "three types of guard personnel":

> The first category of guard is the malicious, nasty, basically evil, vulgar, vile, low-natured type. They see the prisoner as an object upon whom they can unleash their perverted urges, their bad moods, and their inferiority complexes without restraint or fear of resistance. They know neither compassion nor any warm feelings for others. . . . They spend their time thinking up new methods of mental and physical torture. . . .
>
> The second category of guard is the majority. These are the apathetic and indifferent ones who ploddingly perform their duties in a careless or deficient manner and do only what is absolutely necessary. . . . For the most part, their intelligence is somewhat limited. By and large they do not wish to harm the prisoners, but by their indifference, laziness, or limited intelligence, they unintentionally harm, torture, and hurt many prisoners. Above all, they are the ones who make it possible for prisoners to rule over other prisoners, often leading to a disastrous end.
>
> The third category consists of those who by nature are kind, have a good heart, have compassion and empathy for human suffering. However, even here there are vast differences. First there are those who strictly and conscientiously go by the book and do not overlook any breaking of the camp rules by the prisoners, but whose heart and good will interpret the book in favor of the prisoner, who try as much as possible to ease the life of the prisoner, or at least not make it unnecessarily more difficult. There are also those who are too good-hearted, whose naivete sometimes borders on the miraculous. These guards overlook everything as far as the prisoners are concerned and try to fulfill their every wish; to help them where they can because of their good-heartedness and unlimited compassion. They cannot believe that there are evil men among the prisoners.

Apparently Höss classified himself among the latter group in terms of temperament. "My heart was tied to the prisoners because I had suffered their kind of life for too long and had also experienced their needs," he wrote. "I should have gone to [Inspector of the Concentration Camps Theodor] Eicke or [*Reichsführer-SS*] Himmler and explained that I was not suited for service in the concentration camp because I had too much compassion for the prisoners." As overseer of the deaths of more than 2.5 million inmates of Auschwitz, Rudolf Höss somehow managed to suppress his compassion.

kindness and his soft heart clearly came out in the open." Under his new mentor, Höss was promoted to camp executive officer "around Christmas 1939." [122]

But in January 1940, Heinrich Himmler paid a surprise visit to Sachsenhausen that resulted in a change of commandants. Baranowski was replaced by Hans Loritz because "in Himmler's opinion there was no discipline in the camp and that [Loritz] would bring it up to standards." [123] Thereafter, Höss became more convinced than ever of the importance of always maintaining the appearance of toughness.

Höss's call to contemptible command came nine months after the outbreak of World War II. He was promoted to captain (*SS-Hauptsturmführer*) and appointed commandant of Auschwitz on May 1, 1940, a position he would hold until December 1, 1943.

"During his three and a half years at Auschwitz," writes Robert S. Wistrich, "Höss proved himself the ideal type of the passionless, disinterested mass murderer, the quiet bureaucrat who never personally attended selections for the gas chambers or mass executions." Höss appeared to be "a kindly, unselfish, introverted family man and animal lover" who "took a perfectionist pride in his 'work.'" According to Wistrich:

It was Höss, the perfect example of the conscientious, self-disciplined, petty-bourgeois [lower-middle-class] auto-maton whose golden rule was "Only one thing is valid; orders!", who ensured the smooth functioning of the extermination system at Auschwitz, treating mass murder as a purely administrative procedure. What concerned Höss was not the indescribable suffering of his victims but rather the practical difficulties of carrying out his assignment with maximum efficiency—questions involving the precise adherence to timetables, the size of transports, the types of oven and methods of gassing. He took pride in being the first to utilize successfully "Zyklon B"—the squeamish Höss, who could not bear shootings and bloodshed, found gas to be infinitely more rational, bloodless and hygienic. Höss's sense of duty, his absolute submission to authority, his conscientious adherence to the SS motto "Believe! Obey! Fight!" immunized him to any emotion except that of self-pity.[124]

(Left to right) Rudolf Brandt, Heinrich Himmler, Max Faust, and Rudolf Höss tour the construction of Auschwitz. A passionless individual with a dedication to following orders, Höss was concerned not by the deaths of his Jewish prisoners but merely with how to efficiently carry out their destruction.

"No Reason to Complain"

Perhaps the question most frequently asked of the overseers and dispensers of death in Nazi Germany's killing camps was, "How can you stand watching people die day after day?" In *Death Dealer: The Memoirs of the SS Kommandant at Auschwitz*, Rudolf Höss answered the question from the perspective of one of history's worst mass killers:

> I had to do all of this [continually witness the executions] because I was the one to whom everyone looked, and because I had to show everybody that I was not only the one who gave the orders and issued the directives, but that I was also willingly to be present at whatever task I ordered my men to perform.

> Himmler sent various high-ranking Party officials and SS officers to Auschwitz to see the process of the extermination of the Jews. All of them were deeply impressed by what they saw. Some of them who had lectured before very fanatically about the necessity of this extermination became completely silent while viewing the "Final Solution of the Jewish Question" and remained so. I was asked repeatedly how I and my men could watch these proceedings day after day. How we could stand it? I gave the same answer time and again, that only iron determination could carry out Hitler's orders and this could only be achieved by stifling all human emotion. Even [SS general of the Gestapo] Mildner and Eichmann, who had a reputation of being truly hard, said they would not want to change places with me. No one envied me my job. . . .

> And yet, I really had no reason to complain about being bored at Auschwitz.

At Auschwitz, Höss carried out his duties so well that an SS report issued in 1944 called him "a true pioneer in this area because of his new ideas and educational methods."[125]

"A Normal Life"

Höss kept himself isolated from the actual killing process as much as possible. But at least on one occasion, he took an active role in the murder of inmates. Historian Martin Gilbert describes his part in the shooting of several female prisoners in 1943:

> On October 23, 1,750 Polish Jews from the group held at Bergen-Belsen were deported to Birkenau [the killing annex at Auschwitz]. There, they were driven into the undressing chamber by SS Sergeant Major Josef Schillinger. A former roll-call leader in the men's camp at Birkenau, Schillinger had become feared and hated for his habit of choking Jews to death while they were eating their meager meals.

> The women were ordered to undress. As they did so, the German guards, as usual, seized rings from fingers and watches from wrists. During this activity, Schillinger himself ordered one of the women to undress completely. This woman, who according to some reports was a former Warsaw dancer by the name of Horowitz, threw her shoe in Schillinger's face, seized his revolver, and shot him in the stomach. She also wounded another SS man, Sergeant Emmerich. The shooting of Schillinger served as a signal for the other women to attack the SS men at the entrance to the gas-chamber. One SS man had his nose torn off, another was scalped.

> Schillinger died on the way to the camp hospital. The other SS man fled. Shortly

"Mausoleums of Horror"

After the U.S. Army 80th Division liberated the Buchenwald concentration camp on April 10, 1945, Hitler ordered *Reichsführer-SS* Heinrich Himmler to ensure against any more camps falling into Allied hands. Furthermore, no camp inmates capable of marching were to be left behind in any camp. This order resulted in forced evacuations. Rudolf Höss testified before the International Military Tribunal in Nuremberg about the removal of inmates from Sachsenhausen. In *Tyranny on Trial: The Evidence at Nuremberg*, former U.S. assistant prosecutor Whitney R. Harris includes the following extracts from Höss's testimony:

> The Gestapo chief, Gruppenführer Müller, called me in the evening and told me that the Reichsführer had ordered that the camp at Sachsenhausen was to be evacuated at once. I pointed out to Gruppenführer Müller what that would mean. Sachsenhausen could no longer fall back on any other camp except perhaps on a few labor camps attached to the armament works that were almost filled up anyway. Most of the internees would have to be sheltered in the woods somewhere. This would mean countless thousands of deaths and, above all, it would be impossible to feed these masses of people. He promised me that he would again discuss these measures with the Reichsführer. He called me back and told me that the Reichsführer had refused and was demanding that the commanders carry out his orders immediately.

"If the concentration camps had been adequately maintained to the moment of surrender great loss of life could have been avoided," Harris notes. "Unfortunately, as the military situation deteriorated it became increasingly difficult to obtain the food and medical supplies required to support the large population of the camps." Höss went on to describe the plight of the inmates:

> The catastrophic situation at the end of the war was due to the fact that, as a result of the destruction of the railway network and the continuous bombing of the industrial plants, care for these masses—I am thinking of Auschwitz with its 140,000 internees—could no longer be assured. Improvised measures, truck columns, and everything else tried by the commanders to improve the situation were of little or no avail; it was no longer possible. The number of the sick became immense. There were next to no medical supplies; epidemics raged everywhere. Internees who were capable of work were used over and over again. By order of the Reichsführer, even half-sick people had to be used wherever possible in industry. As a result, every bit of space in the concentration camps which could possibly be used for lodging was overcrowded with sick and dying prisoners.

Harris concludes:

> In the final days thousands of prisoners died in Dachau and the other concentration camps. Bodies could not be burned because there was neither fuel nor the personnel to operate the crematories. The quick and the dead lay side by side in the tiered barracks, the moaning of the dying and the stench of the corpses creating the mausoleums of horror discovered by the advancing armies of liberation.

afterwards the camp commandant, Rudolf Höss, entered the chamber, accompanied by other SS men carrying machine guns and grenades. They then removed the women one by one, and shot them outside.[126]

Höss may have bloodied his own hands on more than this occasion, but for the most part he stood aside while his minions bloodied theirs. And though he directed and witnessed countless atrocities in the camps, he was still able to say of himself, "I am completely normal. Even while I was carrying out the task of extermination I lived a normal life and so on."[127]

Rudolf Höss is extradited for trial by American occupation forces to Polish authorities in 1946. Höss was hanged in 1947.

Return to Auschwitz

On November 22, 1943, the single command of the Auschwitz-Birkenau complex, including some thirty-odd subcamps, was divided into three separate command groups. Oswald Pohl, chief of the SS Economic and Administrative Main Office (WVHA), offered Höss the choice of becoming either commandant of Sachsenhausen or chief of concentration camp inspectors. Höss later recalled:

This was a gesture of goodwill on his part for what I had accomplished at Auschwitz. At first I was not happy about moving away because Auschwitz had become my life precisely because of the difficulties, the problems, and the many difficult duties. But afterward, I was glad that I was free from all of it. I had had enough after nine years of general service in concentration camps and three-and-a-half years at Auschwitz.[128]

Höss chose to become chief of concentration camp inspectors. In 1945, at Martin Bormann's recommendation, Höss was elevated to serve as deputy to General (*SS-Obergruppenführer*) Richard Glücks, head of the inspectorate of concentration camps. Höss served out the remainder of the war in that capacity.

On March 11, 1946, the British Field Security Police arrested Höss near Flensburg, a seaport on the Baltic in northern Germany, and turned him over to Polish authorities about two weeks later. Thirteen months thereafter, Rudolf Franz Höss—the death dealer of Auschwitz, who personally oversaw the murders of some 2.5 million souls—answered for his crimes before a military tribunal in Warsaw. The tribunal found him guilty and sentenced him to death on March 27, 1947.

Höss's sentence was carried out on April 7, 1947. He was hanged inside the camp at Auschwitz, next to the house where he had lived with his wife and five children.

Josef Mengele: Angel of Death

Anne Frank called Dr. Josef Mengele, the chief camp doctor at the Auschwitz death camp, "the angel of extermination."[129] A prisoner/doctor once said of him:

> He was capable of being so kind to the children, to have them become fond of him, to bring them sugar, to think of small details in their daily lives, and to do things we would genuinely admire. . . . And then, next to that . . . the crematoria smoke, and these children, tomorrow or in a half-hour, he is going to send them there. Well, that is where the anomaly lay.[130]

During a 1982 interview, European journalist Gita Sereny asked Hans Münch, a German doctor who had served under Mengele at Auschwitz, about his former chief. Sereny describes Münch as having been "an extraordinary young German doctor" who "appeared unable to condemn the monstrous Mengele, who, to him, was not a monster."[131] Of Mengele, Münch said:

> He was exceptionally knowledgeable about medicine. From the scientific point of view, he was the only SS doctor there of quality. For me, he was very worth talking with.
>
> He was an ideologue [idealist or visionary], body and soul. Never any emotion; he

showed no hate or fanaticism. And in this way he saw the gassings as the only rational solution, and as the Jews were going to die anyway, he saw no reason not to use them first for medical experiments.

> [Even though Münch did not agree with Mengele's "monstrous reasoning," he said that] he fascinated me. He was entirely unique. I found his mind irresistible. I have to admit that I wanted to be with him, sought him out, so I cannot now claim that I didn't like him.[132]

The Auschwitz career of Dr. Josef Mengele represents a case study in coldhearted clinical savagery that stands horrifically absolute and unique in the practice of medicine. Psychiatrist Robert Jay Lifton, in his scholarly study of the Nazi doctors, characterizes physicians as "healers" who "work at the border of life and death." He further defines the Nazi killing programs as "medicalized killing" and the doctors who took part in them as "healers-turned-killers."[133] No one more exemplifies the latter term than Dr. Josef Mengele.

Assignment at Auschwitz

Josef Mengele was born on March 16, 1911, in Günzburg, Bavaria, the son of a Bavarian farm equipment manufacturer. While studying

German physician Josef Mengele used his position during the Holocaust to perform gruesome human experiments, especially on identical twins.

philosophy in Munich during the 1920s, Mengele became enamored of the racial ideology of Alfred Rosenberg. He grew to accept Rosenberg's Aryan theory as scientific truth. In Munich, he also met Hitler and became a dedicated follower of the future führer.

An outstanding student of high intellect, Mengele eventually earned two doctorates. He took his first doctorate in physical anthropology at Munich under Theodor Mollison in 1935; his second, in medicine at Frankfurt under Otmar Freiherr von Verschuer in 1938. Both of his doctoral dissertations dealt with research in racial hygiene. After taking his medical degree and receiving his license to practice medicine, he elected to enter the field of medical research

rather than to pursue a medical specialty.

At Verschuer's Frankfurt Institute for Hereditary Biology and Race Hygiene, Mengele cultivated a theory that humans, like dogs and cats, have pedigrees. From this premise, he would later begin experiments aimed at breeding a super race of blond, blue-eyed Nordic giants. In 1938, working under research grants from the German Research Foundation (*Deutsche Forschungsgemeinschaft*, or DFG), Verschuer reported to the DFG on research involving the genetic study of twins. His report listed the contributions and publications of his assistant, Dr. Josef Mengele.

Commissioned a second lieutenant (*SS-Untersturmführer*) in the Waffen-SS (the military arm of the SS) in 1939, Mengele served as a medical officer in France and Russia. In May 1943 Heinrich Himmler appointed Mengele, by then a captain (*SS-Hauptsturmführer*), chief doctor at Auschwitz. In addition to the routine duties of a concentration camp physician, his new assignment required him to direct selections for the gas chamber. Each day, dressed always in a spotlessly white medical coat, he greeted incoming truck- or trainloads of new arrivals and directed each person either "Right!" (work squads) or "Left!" (gas chambers). Because of Mengele's immaculate appearance and his power of life and death over camp inmates, the prisoners referred to him as the "Angel of Death."[134]

It is thought that Mengele asked to be sent to Auschwitz because of the opportunities the camp could provide for his genetic research, especially on twins. In any case, as Henry Friedlander, professor of history at Brooklyn College of the City University of New York, points out:

Auschwitz opened up unlimited opportunities for an ambitious researcher. Research

Auschwitz, Arias, and Atrocities

Dr. Josef Mengele's assignment to Auschwitz provided him with the opportunity and setting to perform his bizarre medical experiments without sanction or interference. Authors Lucette Matalon Lagnado and Sheila Cohn Dekel, in *Children of the Flames: Dr. Josef Mengele and the Untold Story of the Twins of Auschwitz*, sketch a disquieting picture of Mengele's "research" environment:

What is universally known today as Auschwitz is in fact something of a misnomer. Auschwitz was the slave-labor camp in which murder was an everyday phenomenon, but, in fact, the Polish place name became the umbrella word for several camps. Although the slaves labored largely at Auschwitz, it was at Birkenau, a couple of miles away, that many of them were executed. And although the world lexicon came to equate Auschwitz with the gas chambers, it was Birkenau that was the actual extermination center. It was Birkenau where the ovens never stopped flaming and where SS physicians regularly dispatched inmates to the crematorium; and it was Birkenau where Dr. Mengele worked in his laboratory, and where his beloved twins were barracked, and where so many of them inevitably perished.

Just one year after arriving at the death camp, Mengele was thoroughly absorbed in his research, the first step of which was selecting his subjects. Every morning, at the crack of dawn, he could be seen in the area where the transports disembarked, scanning the new arrivals.

Standing there in his perfectly tailored SS uniform, white gloves, and officer's cap, Mengele looked impeccable—a host greeting guests arriving at his home. He sometimes stood for hours without flinching, a hint of a smile on his face, his elegantly gloved hand beckoning the prisoners to the right or to the left. Often, he whistled softly as he worked, the *Blue Danube* waltz, or an aria from his favorite Puccini opera.

Mengele even engaged some of the new arrivals in friendly conversation, asking them how the journey had been, and how they were feeling. If they complained of being sick, he listened with a sympathetic ear—and then sent them straightaway to die in the gas chambers. He actually seemed interested in hearing all the gruesome details: how uncomfortable the trip had been, how cramped and stifling the cattle cars were, how many Jews died along the way.

Occasionally, Mengele pulled aside inmates and asked them to write "postcards" to their relatives back home. He seemed to take a special pleasure in dictating these notes, describing how lovely Auschwitz was, and urging everyone to visit. But once the postcards were prepared, their authors were summarily dispatched to the gas chambers.

Only when an interesting "specimen" came along did Mengele really spring to life. He urgently motioned to a nearby guard to yank the new arrival out of line. SS guards were ordered to watch for any unusual or striking genetic material—the dwarfs, the giants, the hunchbacks—and to bring them immediately to Mengele. But most important of all to him were the twins.

subjects were available in large numbers, and the restraints of medical ethics did not apply. Further, Mengele could compel highly skilled inmate physicians to design and conduct research, perform tests and autopsies, and produce research papers, without the need to share credit with them. It is therefore not surprising that Mengele used Auschwitz as a research laboratory.[135]

Meanwhile, Otmar von Verschuer, Mengele's old mentor, had moved to Berlin to succeed Eugen Fischer as director of the Kaiser Wilhelm Institute for Anthropology. Mengele worked at the institute when SS assignments occasionally brought him to Berlin. He thereby continued his contributions to Verschuer's research projects, which enabled Verschuer to carry Mengele's later work at Auschwitz on his DFG grants. According to Professor Friedlander, when Mengele began genetic experiments on various racial groups at Auschwitz, he sent blood samples to Verschuer for testing:

Mengele mailed the results of his research on Jewish and Gypsy twins to the Kaiser Wilhelm Institute. There scientists analyzed the samples of blood obtained before death and the organs obtained after dissection. Mengele's investigation of eye color was only one bizarre example of such criminal experiments. He collected

Jews arrive at Auschwitz in 1944. Mengele was responsible for selecting which inmates would be assigned to work squads and which would be condemned to the gas chambers.

pairs of eyes if one of the pair had a different color, hoping that he could discover ways to change eye color. At one time, Mengele killed an entire Gypsy family to send their eyes for analysis to Karin Magnussen at Kaiser Wilhelm Institute.[136]

As an unprincipled medical researcher, Mengele could scarcely have asked or wanted for more than an assignment at Auschwitz.

Psychiatrist Robert Jay Lifton asserts that Mengele brought a "murderous scientific fanaticism"[137] to Auschwitz. Elaborating on Lifton's assertion, historian Klaus P. Fischer writes, "Yet his [Mengele's] murderous activities were conducted within constraints of fanatical order and with mind-numbing pedantry, for, according to him, this research had a noble purpose, namely to breed a higher form of human being."[138] Polish doctor Martina Puzyna, who was forced to assist Mengele, validates the views of both Lifton and Fischer:

I found Mengele a picture of what can only be described as a maniac. He turned the truth on its head. He believed you could create a new super-race as though you were breeding horses. He thought it was possible to gain control over a whole race. . . . He was a racist and a Nazi. He was ambitious up to the point of being completely inhuman. He was mad about genetic engineering. I believe he thought that when he'd finished with the Jewish race, he'd start on the Poles, and when he'd finished with them, he'd start on someone else. Above all, I believe he was doing this . . . for his career. In the end I believed that he would have killed his own mother if it would have helped him.[139]

"If in ordinary times [Mengele] would probably have been a slightly sadistic German professor, as one colleague speculated, Auschwitz transformed him into the archetype of Nazi evil," Fischer adds. "In the eyes of his Jewish victims he became the embodiment of their deepest collective fears—the key to their 'sense of fear of everything that is German.'"[140]

Premature Postmortem

The only children spared from the gas chambers at Auschwitz were twins, since much of Mengele's unconscionable research was focused on them. Mengele personally selected all twins, children and adults alike, and assigned them to special barracks to become subjects for his experiments. He experimented on some fifteen hundred Jewish twins during the eighteen months after his arrival in Auschwitz in late May 1943. Fewer than two hundred survived.

Forty years later, Vera Kriegel, one of the survivors, remembered that Mengele was directing the selection process when she and her then five-year-old twin sister, Olga, arrived at Auschwitz. A flick of his finger to the right or to the left sent those selected either to a slow death in a labor camp or to a quick death in a crematorium. Vera recalled:

Children were having their heads beaten in like poultry by SS men with their gun butts and some were being thrown into a smoking pit. I was confused: I thought that this was some sort of animal kingdom or perhaps I was already in Hell.

Their father was among those fingered for death, but the twins and their mother survived. Their lives were spared, as Vera Kriegel later explained to a Jerusalem court, because Mengele "wanted to know why our eyes were brown while our mother's were blue." Mengele forced the twins to live in a straw-covered cage for ten days, while he conducted his bizarre experiments. "They injected our eyes with liquid that burnt," Vera said. "But we tried to remain strong, because we knew that in Auschwitz the weak went 'up the chimney.'"[141]

Writes historian Martin Gilbert:

Among the Jews who died as a result of Mengele's experiments were two Hungarian twins on whom Mengele had performed head surgery, a thirty-year-old Jewish woman from Szombathely whose twin sister was also killed by

---

"Mengele Is God"

The study of the genetic characteristics of twins fascinated Dr. Josef Mengele like those of no other subjects of his so-called scientific research. Thus, many twins received special consideration from Mengele—who held the power of life or death over them—and survived Auschwitz to tell their sordid tales. In his landmark study *The Nazi Doctors: Medical Killing and the Psychology of Genocide*, eminent psychiatrist Robert Jay Lifton illustrates Mengele's omnipotence through the recollections of Auschwitz survivors:

> Within the Auschwitz twins' subculture, there was an odd atmosphere that combined sanctuary with terror. As Simon J. [a pseudonym] put it, twins got the message "If we do what is wanted from us, . . . we would come to no harm, because we are the subject of an investigation headed by Dr. Mengele." That is, "We were not allowed to be beaten" because the word was out "not to ruin us physically.". . . Even a twin who was caught in such an ordinarily "ultimate sin" as stealing food would, instead of being severely beaten or sent to the gas chambers, be merely rebuked or punished mildly. The twins became aware that, unlike most other prisoners, their lives had existential value: "A single thing kept us [alive]: . . . his experiments," is the way Tomas A. [another pseudonym] put it. Their existential value was immediately apparent in the matter of hair: they could retain theirs for

the research reason that hair characteristics, including color, had to be recorded.

> Hence they were given desirable jobs that did not expose them to the most severe kinds of physical abuse; children among them could serve as a "runner" (*Läufer*) or messenger, or sometimes simply as a helper. Many were permitted relatively freely about the camp, and therefore had valuable opportunities for "organizing" (buying and selling, mostly food), to be privy to useful information, and to create what one of them called a "thriving economy" on the twin block [housing quarters].

> They were rewarded for their cooperation, as A. tells us: "[After being] measured and measured, . . . we had white bread and . . . milk with *Lukchen* [a macaroni-like mixture, considered a great delicacy in the camp]," for the ostensible purpose of compensating for the blood that had to be taken from them. In the Auschwitz context, that was "marvelous," and was combined with other advantages: "the best clothes . . . through Mengele"; and as a survivor twin explained, "We had our hair . . . [so] they [other prisoners] said, 'At least, you look . . . human.'"

> It was equally clear, however, that this sanctuary was more than a matter of Mengele's whim: As Simon J. put it, "Mengele is God—we found it out very fast."

Mengele or on his orders to allow for a comparative autopsy, and a one-year-old triplet from Munkacs on whom Mengele was said to have conducted a 'post-mortem' [autopsy] under anaesthesis while the child was still alive.[142]

Killer Angel

Mengele killed the subjects of his experiments without reservation or remorse. "In many instances, amounting over a year and a half to several thousand, Mengele used the pretext of medical treatment to kill prisoners," purports Martin Gilbert, "injecting them with phenol, petrol, chloroform or air, or by ordering SS orderlies to do so."[143]

In a deposition made in 1945, Dr. Miklos Nyiszli, a Hungarian inmate and Mengele's main prisoner pathologist, attested to Mengele's capacity for direct murder:

In the work room next to the dissecting room, fourteen Gypsy twins were waiting [about midnight one night], guarded by SS men, and crying bitterly. Dr. Mengele didn't say a single word to us, and prepared a 10 cc. and 5 cc. syringe. From a box he took evipan, and from another

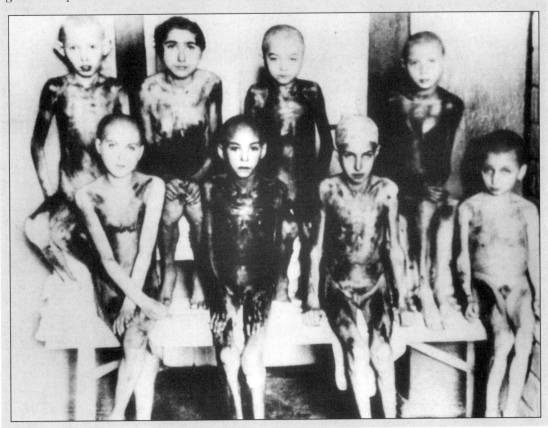

These children from Auschwitz were severely burned during one of Mengele's many pointless and gruesome experiments.

box he took chloroform, which was in 20 cubic-centimeter glass containers, and put these on the operating table. After that, the first twin was brought in, . . . a fourteen-year-old girl. Dr. Mengele ordered me to undress the girl and put her on the dissecting table. Then he injected the evipan into her right arm intravenously. After the child had fallen asleep, he felt for the left ventricle of the heart and injected 10 cc. of chloroform. After one little twitch the child was dead, whereupon Dr. Mengele had it taken into the morgue. In this manner, all fourteen twins were killed during the night.[144]

Alex Dekel, a thirteen-year-old Jewish inmate whom Mengele spared because of his strikingly "Aryan" features, later re-counted his impressions of Auschwitz's killer angel:

I have never accepted the fact that Mengele himself believed he was doing serious medical work—not from the slipshod way he went about it. He was only exercising his power.

Mengele ran a butcher shop—major surgeries were performed without anesthesia. Once, I witnessed a stomach operation—Mengele was removing pieces from the stomach, but without any anesthesia.

Another time, it was a heart that was removed, again, without anesthesia. It was horrifying.

Mengele was a doctor who became mad because of the power he was given. Nobody ever questioned him—why did this one die? Why did that one perish? The patients did not count.

He professed to do what he did in the name of science, but it was a madness on his part.[145]

On another occasion, when a block in the camp was reported infested with lice, Mengele resolved the problem by gassing all 750 of the women residing in it. Maximilian Sternol, a seventy-one-year-old witness of still another incident, later testified:

On the night of July 31, 1944, there were terrible scenes at the liquidation of the Gypsy compound. Women and children were on their knees in front of Mengele and [guard Wilhelm] Boger crying, "Take pity on us,

After the war, many of the camp's prisoner-doctors who were forced to assist Mengele (pictured) delivered evidence against him.

"The Most Monstrous Secret"

Following their invasion of Hungary in March 1944, the Nazis sent virtually the entire Jewish population to Auschwitz. Dr. Miklos Nyiszli, a Jew and a doctor of medicine, was one of more than a million Hungarian Jews slated for death. As a prisoner/doctor Nyiszli's life was spared when he was named Dr. Josef Mengele's personal research pathologist and compelled to perform "scientific research" on his fellow inmates. In *Auschwitz: A Doctor's Eyewitness Account*, Nyiszli describes what he found during the dissection of a set of twins under ten years old, one of many such autopsies that he was forced to perform:

> I began the dissection . . . and recorded each phase of my work. I removed the brain pan. Together with the cerebellum I extracted the brain and examined them. Then followed the opening of the thorax and the removal of the sternum. Next I separated the tongue by means of an incision made beneath the chin. With the tongue came the esophagus, with the respiratory tract came both lungs. I washed the organs in order to examine them more thoroughly. The tiniest spot or the slightest difference in color could furnish valuable information. I made a transverse incision across the pericardium and removed the fluid. Next I took out the heart and washed it. I turned it over and over in my hand to examine it.

> In the exterior coat of the left ventricle was a small pale red spot caused by a hypodermic injection, which scarcely differed from the color of the tissue around it. The injection had been given with a very small needle. Without a doubt a hypodermic needle. For what purpose had he received the injection. Injections into the heart can be administered in extremely serious cases, when the heart begins to fail. I would soon know. I opened the heart, starting with the ventricle. Normally the blood contained in the left ventricle is taken out and weighed. This method could not be employed in the present case, because the blood was coagulated into a compact mass. I extracted the coagulum with the forceps and brought it to my nose. I was struck by the characteristic odor of chloroform. The victim had received an injection of chloroform in the heart, so that the blood of the ventricle, in coagulating, would deposit on the valves and cause instantaneous death by heart failure.

> My discovery of the most monstrous secret of the Third Reich's medical science made my knees tremble. Not only did they kill with gas, but also with injections of chloroform into the heart. . . .

> On several occasions I had been shocked by my discoveries, but now a shudder of fear ran through me. If Dr. Mengele had any idea that I had discovered the secret of his injections he would send ten doctors, in the name of the political SS, to attest to my death.

Dr. Nyiszli did not document his discovery of the chloroform injection in his pathology report and thereby lived to bear future witness to Mengele's atrocities.

take pity on us!" Nothing helped. They were beaten down, brutally trampled upon, and pushed on the trucks. It was a terrible, gruesome sight.[146]

"Mengele also shot a number of prisoners and was reported to have killed at least one by pressing his foot on a woman's body," notes Robert Jay Lifton. "And there were additional reports of his having thrown newborn babies directly into the crematoria or open fires." Whether selecting people for death or killing them himself, the killer angel of Auschwitz displayed "flamboyant detachment—one might say disinterestedness—and efficiency."[147]

Evidence of Mengele's Death

At the end of the war, Mengele was briefly interned in American custody but managed to flee to Buenos Aires under the name of Gregorio Gregori. He thereafter avoided an unrelenting manhunt by Interpol, Israeli agents, and famed Nazi-hunter Simon Wiesenthal for several decades.

More than four decades later, author Alan Levy, Wiesenthal's biographer, visited "the scene of Mengele's crimes at Auschwitz-Birkenau" and "found only a handful of traces of his deadly work: a detailed packing list (signed by him) which had accompanied

Mengele eluded capture after the war. In 1985, Brazilian officials exhumed a corpse thought to be Mengele's. Sixteen forensic scientists confirmed that the corpse was probably the infamous "Angel of Death."

the head of a twelve-year-old gypsy boy that was shipped on 29 June 1944 to a research institute in Germany for further analysis; a photo of four gypsies he'd castrated; several pages of 'anthropological measurements,' and a letter of recommendation from the SS garrison commander at Auschwitz to the Chief Doctor's Office." The note, dated August 19, 1944, states:

Dr. Mengele has been here since 30 May 1943.

Dr. Mengele has an open, honorable, firm character. He is absolutely trustworthy, upright, and direct. His mental and bodily hygiene is outstanding. His appearance indicates no weakness of character, no inclinations or addictions. His intellectual and physical predispositions can be designated as excellent.

In his function as camp physician at Concentration Camp Auschwitz, he applied his knowledge practically and theoretically while fighting grave epidemics. He seized every opportunity, even under difficult circumstances, to improve both his theoretical and practical knowledge. He uses his spare time to search for further opportunities and unusual anthropological materials.

"There are only two pictures of Mengele in the archive: SS identification portraits, neither of them from Auschwitz," adds Levy. "For all his vanity, he rarely let anyone photograph him because he knew he would one day be held responsible for his crimes against the human race."[148]

In 1985 human remains disinterred at Embu, Brazil, were unanimously declared by sixteen forensic scientists to be those of Mengele "within a reasonable scientific certainty."[149] Despite the scientific evidence of Mengele's death, some of his pursuers and surviving former victims cannot dispel the feeling that the killer angel of Auschwitz still lives.

Crimes and Punishments

The world will never know precisely how many Nazi war criminals plied their killing crafts during the Holocaust of World War II, but they must certainly number in the thousands. It hardly seems likely that the slaughter of more than six million Jews could have been accomplished solely by the Nazi leadership corps without the willing—if not enthusiastic—cooperation of thousands of ordinary Germans. As to the cooperation of ordinary Germans, Daniel Jonah Goldhagen, assistant professor of government and social studies at Harvard University, contends:

> The Nazi leadership, like other genocidal elites, never applied, and most likely would not have been willing to apply, the vast amount of coercion that it would have needed to move tens of thousands of non-antisemitic Germans to kill millions of Jews. The Nazis, knowing that ordinary Germans shared their convictions, had no need to do so.
>
> The Holocaust was a *sui generis* [unique] event that has a historically specific explanation. The explanation specifies the enabling conditions created by the long-incubating, pervasive, virulent, racist, eliminationist antisemitism of German culture, which was mobilized by

a criminal regime beholden to an eliminationist, genocidal ideology, and which was given shape and energized by a leader, Hitler, who was adored by the vast majority of the German people, a leader who was known to be committed wholeheartedly to the unfolding, brutal, eliminationist program. During the Nazi period, the eliminationist antisemitism provided the motivational source for the German leadership and for the rank-and-file Germans to kill the Jews. It was also the motivational source of the other non-killing actions of the perpetrators that were integral to the Holocaust.[150]

Given the validity of Goldhagen's contention—which, though arguable, seems likely—logic tells us that thousands of ordinary Germans willingly took part in the war crimes for which far fewer Germans were prosecuted. But guilt by deduction does not equate with guilt proven before a court of law.

Judgment at Nuremberg

In the troubled aftermath of World War II, the victorious Allies faced the difficult problem of what to do with the Nazis who had deliberately slaughtered more than six million Jews and countless others in killings

Nazi soldiers laugh at a Jew forced to dig his own grave. This was a popular amusement of German soldiers conducting mass executions.

unrelated to military needs. Common sense foretold of the difficulty—no, impossibility—of proving the guilt of hundreds of thousands of ordinary Germans; therefore, the Allies did the next best thing: They prosecuted the Nazi war criminals on a selective basis, largely determined by the weight of evidence that could be brought to bear against those selected.

The first defendants indicted by the Allies comprised twenty-two major Nazi war criminals. They were tried on two or more of four counts before the International Military Tribunal during the first phase of the Nuremberg trials. The IMT rendered the following verdicts:

- Hermann Göring: Guilty on all four counts. Sentence: Hanging. Committed suicide several hours before his scheduled execution.

- Rudolf Hess: Guilty on counts one and two. Sentence: Life imprisonment. Hanged himself in Spandau Prison in 1987 at the age of ninety-three.

- Joachim von Ribbentrop: Guilty on all four counts. Sentence: Hanging.

- Wilhelm Keitel: Guilty on all four counts. Sentence: Hanging.

- Ernst Kaltenbrunner: Guilty on counts three and four. Sentence: Hanging.

- Alfred Rosenberg: Guilty on all four counts. Sentence: Hanging.

- Hans Frank: Guilty on counts three and four. Sentence: Hanging.

- Wilhelm Frick: Guilty on counts two, three, and four. Sentence: Hanging.

- Julius Streicher: Guilty on count four. Sentence: Hanging.

- Walther Funk: Guilty on counts two, three, and four. Sentence: Life. Released in 1957 due to illness.

- Hjalmar Schacht: Acquitted of counts one and two.

- Karl Dönitz: Guilty on counts two and three. Sentence: Ten years.

- Erich Raeder: Guilty on counts one, two, and three. Sentence: Life, but released in 1955.

- Baldur von Schirach: Guilty on count four. Sentence: twenty years.

The war criminals' dock at Nuremberg. The Nuremberg trials were the first hearings in which military officials were tried for war crimes.

- Fritz Sauckel: Guilty on counts three and four. Sentence: Hanging.

- Alfred Jodl: Guilty on all four counts. Sentence: Hanging.

- Martin Bormann: Tried in absentia. Guilty on counts three and four. Sentence: Hanging.

- Franz von Papen: Acquitted of counts one and two.

- Artur Seyss-Inquart: Guilty on counts two, three, and four. Sentence: Hanging.

- Albert Speer: Guilty on counts three and four. Sentence: Twenty years.

- Konstantin von Neurath: Guilty on all four counts. Sentence: Fifteen years.

- Hans Fritzsche: Acquitted of counts one, three, and four.

Of seven Nazi organizations indicted, the tribunal rendered a criminal judgment against the Nazi Party leadership, the SS, the Gestapo, and the SD. Members of these four organizations were thus guilty of crimes by association. The SA, the Reich cabinet, and the High Command were acquitted of guilt.

The death sentences, except for those of Göring and Bormann, were carried out on October 16, 1946, on three temporary gallows in the Nuremberg Prison gymnasium.

The Legacy of Nuremberg

The second phase of the Nuremberg proceedings began in November 1946 and lasted until April 1949. The Americans organized the follow-on hearings into twelve separate trials under their sole jurisdiction. These trials decided the fate of an

Former Gestapo officer Klaus Barbie stands trial in Lyons, France, in 1987 for crimes committed in that city while it was under Nazi occupation.

additional 185 defendants, of which 35 were acquitted, 19 were further released on various grounds, 24 were executed, 20 were sentenced to life in prison, and 87 were dealt shorter terms of imprisonment.

Overall, trials held in the American, British, and French zones between 1945 and 1949 resulted in the conviction and punishment of some 5,025 Germans.

In the ensuing decades, additional trials have been held—and continue to be held—throughout Europe and in Israel in the so-called third phase of war crimes trials. Notable among the third-phase trials are those of Adolf Eichmann and John Demjanjuk in Jerusalem and Klaus Barbie in Lyons, France.

In 1962 an Israeli court found Eichmann guilty and sentenced him to hang. Demjanjuk, accused of being the notorious "Ivan the Terrible" who operated the gas chamber at Treblinka, was found guilty by another Israel court in 1988. Demjanjuk was released in 1993, however, after new evidence raised doubts about his identification. In 1987 Barbie, the head of the SD and Gestapo in France, known as the "Butcher of Lyons," was convicted by a French court and sentenced to life imprisonment. Barbie has since died in prison.

War crimes trials will assuredly continue to be held until the last Nazi war criminal is either brought to justice or lies deep in his grave—for that is the legacy of Nuremberg.

Notes

Introduction: Of Courts, Crimes, and Criminals

1. Louis L. Snyder, *Encyclopedia of the Third Reich*. New York: Paragon House, 1989, p. 84.

2. Quoted in Richard Breitman, *The Architect of Genocide: Himmler and the Final Solution*. New York: Knopf, 1991, p. 18.

3. Snyder, *Encyclopedia of the Third Reich*, p. 254.

4. Snyder, *Encyclopedia of the Third Reich*, p. 254.

5. Gita Sereny, *Albert Speer: His Battle with Truth*. New York: Knopf, 1995, p. 682.

6. Klaus P. Fischer, *Nazi Germany: A New History*. New York: The Continuum, 1995, p. 513.

7. Fischer, *Nazi Germany*, p. 486.

8. Quoted in Fischer, *Nazi Germany*, p. 512.

9. Fischer, *Nazi Germany*, pp. 512–13.

10. Fischer, *Nazi Germany*, p. 485.

Chapter 1: Heinrich Himmler: Architect of Genocide

11. Breitman, *The Architect of Genocide*, p. 1.

12. Quoted in Gerald Reitlinger, *The SS: Alibi of a Nation, 1922–1945*. New York: Da Capo Press, 1989, p. 278.

13. Reitlinger, *The SS*, p. 278.

14. Quoted in John Toland, *Adolf Hitler*. New York: Anchor Books (Doubleday), 1992, p. 768.

15. Quoted in Rupert Butler, *An Illustrated History of the Gestapo*. London: Wordwright Books, 1996, p. 32.

16. Quoted in Breitman, *The Architect of Genocide*, pp. 5–6.

17. Quoted in Snyder, *Encyclopedia of the Third Reich*, p. 98.

18. Quoted in G. S. Graber, *The History of the SS*. New York: David McKay, 1978, p. 12.

19. Butler, *An Illustrated History of the Gestapo*, p. 21.

20. Quoted in the Editors of Time-Life Books, *The SS*, vol. 2 of The Third Reich series. Alexandria, VA: Time-Life Books, 1989, p. 20.

21. Quoted in Graber, *The History of the SS*, p. 18.

22. Butler, *An Illustrated History of the Gestapo*, p. 38.

23. Graber, *The History of the SS*, p. 18.

24. Quoted in Butler, *An Illustrated History of the Gestapo*, p. 38.

25. Quoted in Butler, *An Illustrated History of the Gestapo*, p. 39.

26. Graber, *The History of the SS*, p. 18.

27. Butler, *An Illustrated History of the Gestapo*, p. 43.

28. Quoted in Graber, *The History of the SS*, pp. 18–19.

29. Quoted in Peter Padfield, *Himmler: Reichsführer-SS*. New York: Henry Holt, Owl Books, 1993, p. 101.

30. Quoted in Padfield, *Himmler*, p. 127.

31. Quoted in Reitlinger, *The SS*, p. 90.

32. Snyder, *Encyclopedia of the Third Reich*, p. 147.

33. Quoted in Reitlinger, *The SS*, p. 275.

34. Quoted in Lucy S. Dawidowicz, *The War Against the Jews, 1933–1945*. New York: Bantam Books, 1986, p. 120.

35. Quoted in Abraham J. Edelheit and Hershel Edelheit, *History of the Holocaust: A Handbook and Dictionary*. Boulder, CO: Westview Press, 1994, p. 224.

36. Quoted in Padfield, *Himmler*, p. 598.

37. Quoted in Snyder, *Encyclopedia of the Third Reich*, p. 148.

Chapter 2: Julius Streicher: "Jew-Baiter Number One"

38. Quoted in I. C. B. Dear and M. R. D. Foot, eds., *The Oxford Companion to World War II*. New York: Oxford University Press, 1995, p. 1,079.

39. Quoted in Martin Gilbert, *The Holocaust: A History of the Jews of Europe During the Second World War*, New York: Henry Holt, Owl Books, 1987, p. 25.

40. William L. Shirer, *The Rise and Fall of the Third Reich*. New York: Simon & Schuster, 1960, p. 50.

41. Shirer, *The Rise and Fall of the Third Reich*, p. 50.

42. Toland, *Adolf Hitler*, p. 125.

43. Shirer, *The Rise and Fall of the Third Reich*, p. 26.

44. Fischer, *Nazi Germany*, p. 135.

45. Snyder, *Encyclopedia of the Third Reich*, p. 336.

46. Robert S. Wistrich, *Who's Who in Nazi Germany*. New York: Routledge, 1995, pp. 250–51.

47. Quoted in Robert E. Conot, *Justice at Nuremberg*. New York: Carroll & Graf, 1994, p. 382.

48. Quoted in Wistrich, *Who's Who in Nazi Germany*, p. 251.

49. Quoted in Toland, *Adolf Hitler*, p. 126.

50. Quoted in Snyder, *Encyclopedia of the Third Reich*, p. 337.

51. Quoted in Whitney R. Harris, *Tyranny on Trial: The Evidence at Nuremberg*. New York: Barnes & Noble, 1995, p. 283.

52. Quoted in Snyder, *Encyclopedia of the Third Reich*, p. 337.

53. Anthony Read and David Fisher, *Kristallnacht: The Unleashing of the Holocaust*. New York: Peter Bedrick Books, 1989, p. 101.

54. Read and Fisher, *Kristallnacht*, p. 102.

55. Read and Fisher, *Kristallnacht*, p. 102.

56. William L. Shirer, *Berlin Diary: The Journal of a Foreign Correspondent, 1934–1941*. New York: Galahad Books, 1995, p. 568.

57. Quoted in G. M. Gilbert, *Nuremberg Diary*. New York: Da Capo Press, 1995, pp. 442–43.

58. Quoted in Conot, *Justice at Nuremberg*, p. 505.

59. Quoted in Joseph E. Persico, *Nuremberg: Infamy on Trial*. New York: Penguin Books, 1995, pp. 426–27.

60. Quoted in Telford Taylor, *The Anatomy of the Nuremberg Trials*. Boston: Little, Brown, 1992, p. 610.

Chapter 3: Reinhard Heydrich: God of Death

61. Quoted in Butler, *An Illustrated History of the Gestapo*, p. 121.

62. John Weitz, *Hitler's Diplomat: The Life and Times of Joachim von Ribbentrop*. New York: Ticknor & Fields, 1992, p. 77.

63. Quoted in Callum MacDonald, *The Killing of SS Obergruppenführer Reinhard*

Heydrich. New York: Collier, 1989, p. 5.

64. Quoted in MacDonald, *The Killing of SS Obergruppenführer Reinhard Heydrich*, p. 5.

65. Quoted in MacDonald, *The Killing of SS Obergruppenführer Reinhard Heydrich*, p. 5.

66. Ib Melchoir and Frank Brandenburg, *Quest: Searching for Germany's Nazi Past; a Young Man's Story*. Novato, CA: Presidio Press, 1990, p. 122.

67. Quoted in Butler, *An Illustrated History of the Gestapo*, p. 64.

68. Wistrich, *Who's Who in Nazi Germany*, p. 108.

69. Quoted in Padfield, *Himmler*, p. 243.

70. Padfield, *Himmler*, p. 243.

71. Weitz, *Hitler's Diplomat*, p. 219.

72. Quoted in Weitz, *Hitler's Diplomat*, p. 219.

73. Padfield, *Himmler*, p. 270.

74. Quoted in Fischer, *Nazi Germany*, p. 499.

75. Quoted in Leni Yahil, *The Holocaust: The Fate of European Jewry*, translated by Ina Friedman and Haya Galai. New York: Oxford University Press, 1990, pp. 254–55.

76. Quoted in Snyder, *Encyclopedia of the Third Reich*, p. 372.

77. Quoted in Daniel Jonah Goldhagen, *Hitler's Willing Executioners: Ordinary Germans and the Holocaust*. New York: Knopf, 1996, p. 322.

78. Quoted in Snyder, *Encyclopedia of the Third Reich*, p. 372.

79. Quoted in Goldhagen, *Hitler's Willing Executioners*, p. 323.

80. Quoted in Toland, *Adolf Hitler*, p. 705.

81. Quoted in Wistrich, *Who's Who in Nazi Germany*, p. 110.

82. Quoted in MacDonald, *The Killing of SS Obergruppenführer Reinhard Heydrich*, p. 182.

83. Quoted in Padfield, *Himmler*, p. 380.

84. Alan Levy, *The Wiesenthal File*. Grand Rapids, MI: Eerdmans , 1994, p. 108.

85. Wistrich, *Who's Who in Nazi Germany*, p. 110.

86. Quoted in Snyder, *Encyclopedia of the Third Reich*, p. 145.

Chapter 4: Adolf Eichmann: Grand Inquisitor

87. Quoted in Levy, *The Wiesenthal File*, p. 111.

88. Quoted in Snyder, *Encyclopedia of the Third Reich*, p. 80.

89. Quoted in Hannah Arendt, *Eichmann in Jerusalem: A Report on the Banality of Evil*. New York: Penguin Books, 1977, p. 35.

90. Butler, *An Illustrated History of the Gestapo*, p. 79.

91. Quoted in Levy, *The Wiesenthal File*, p. 96.

92. Robert Edwin Herzstein and the Editors of Time-Life Books, *The Nazis*. Alexandria, VA: Time-Life Books, 1981, p. 143.

93. Herzstein, *The Nazis*, p. 143.

94. Quoted in Arendt, *Eichmann in Jerusalem*, p. 83.

95. Quoted in Arendt, *Eichmann in Jerusalem*, p. 83.

96. Quoted in Levy, *The Wiesenthal File*, p. 107.

97. Rudolf Höss, *Death Dealer: The Memoirs of the SS Kommandant at Auschwitz*, translated by A. Pollinger. New York: Da Capo Press, 1996, pp. 240–41.

98. Wistrich, *Who's Who in Nazi Germany*, p. 50.

99. Quoted in Herzstein, *The Nazis*, p. 143.

100. Quoted in Herzstein , *The Nazis*, p. 143.

101. Höss, *Death Dealer*, pp. 28–29.

102. Wistrich, *Who's Who in Nazi Germany*, pp. 50–51.

103. Quoted in Levy, *The Wiesenthal File*, p. 109.

104. Butler, *An Illustrated History of the Gestapo*, p. 194.

105. Quoted in Arendt, *Eichmann in Jerusalem*, p. 279.

106. Arendt, *Eichmann in Jerusalem*, p. 252.

Chapter 5: Rudolf Höss: Death Dealer

107. Quoted in Höss, *Death Dealer*, p. 27.

108. Quoted in Höss, *Death Dealer*, p. 28.

109. Höss, *Death Dealer*, p. 28.

110. Reitlinger, *The SS*, p. 285.

111. Quoted in Snyder, *Encyclopedia of the Third Reich*, p. 167.

112. Quoted in Padfield, *Himmler*, p. 482.

113. Quoted in Snyder, *Encyclopedia of the Third Reich*, p. 167.

114. Quoted in Harris, *Tyranny on Trial*, p. 337.

115. Höss, *Death Dealer*, p. 50.

116. Quoted by Primo Levi in Foreword to Höss, *Death Dealer*, p. 7.

117. Höss, *Death Dealer*, p. 79.

118. Höss, *Death Dealer*, p. 81.

119. Höss, *Death Dealer*, p. 82.

120. Höss, *Death Dealer*, p. 84.

121. Höss, *Death Dealer*, p. 96.

122. Höss, *Death Dealer*, p. 116.

123. Höss, *Death Dealer*, p. 116.

124. Wistrich, *Who's Who in Nazi Germany*, p. 124.

125. Quoted in Snyder, *Encyclopedia of the Third Reich*, p. 166.

126. Gilbert, *The Holocaust*, pp. 621–22.

127. Quoted in Wistrich, *Who's Who in Nazi Germany*, p. 124.

128. Höss, *Death Dealer*, p. 165.

Chapter 6: Josef Mengele: Angel of Death

129. Quoted in Snyder, *Encyclopedia of the Third Reich*, p. 227.

130. Quoted in Robert Jay Lifton, *The Nazi Doctors: Medical Killing and the Psychology of Genocide*. New York: Basic Books, 1986, p. 337.

131. Sereny, *Albert Speer*, pp. 465, 467.

132. Quoted in Sereny, *Albert Speer*, p. 467.

133. Lifton, *The Nazi Doctors*, pp. 15, 17, 123.

134. Quoted in Dear and Foot, *The Oxford Companion to World War II*, p. 738.

135. Henry Friedlander, *The Origins of Nazi Genocide: From Euthanasia to the Final Solution*. Chapel Hill: University of North Carolina Press, 1995, pp. 134–35.

136. Friedlander, *The Origins of Nazi Genocide*, p. 135.

137. Quoted in Fischer, *Nazi Germany*, p. 516.

138. Fischer, *Nazi Germany*, p. 516.

139. Quoted in Fischer, *Nazi Germany*, p. 516.

140. Fischer, *Nazi Germany*, p. 516.

141. Quoted in Gilbert, *The Holocaust*, p. 687.

142. Gilbert, *The Holocaust*, pp. 687–88.

143. Gilbert, *The Holocaust*, pp. 581–82.

144. Quoted in Lifton, *The Nazi Doctors*, pp. 350–51.

145. Quoted in Lucette Matalon Lagnado and Sheila Conn Dekel, *Children of the Flames: Dr. Josef Mengele and the Untold Story of the Twins of Auschwitz*. New York:

William Morrow, 1991, pp. 69–70.

146. Quoted in Snyder, *Encyclopedia of the Third Reich*, p. 228.

147. Lifton, *The Nazi Doctors*, p. 347.

148. Levy, *The Wiesenthal File*, pp. 217–18.

149. Quoted in Snyder, *Encyclopedia of the Third Reich*, p. 228.

Epilogue: Crimes and Punishments

150. Goldhagen, *Hitler's Willing Executioners*, pp. 418–19.

Glossary

Anschluss: Germany's annexation of Austria in 1938.

Aryanism: Nazi theme of the supremacy of racially pure Nordics.

Cyclon B: Crystallized prussic acid used in several of the death camps to kill Jews and others; also spelled Zyclon or Zyklon.

Die Endlösung: The Final Solution.

Einsatzgruppen: Task forces; SS and police units assigned to the "special task" of killing Jews.

Einsatzkommandos: Killer units of the *Einsatzgruppen*.

Final Solution: Nazi euphemism for the annihilation of the Jews of Europe; *Die Endlösung; see also* Holocaust.

General Government: *Generalgouvernement;* German name for Nazi-occupied Poland.

genocide: The deliberate and systematic destruction of a racial, political, or cultural group.

Gestapo: Secret state police; from *GEheime STAatsPOlizei.*

Holocaust: Name for the physical destruction of six million Jews during World War II; *see also* Final Solution.

Judenfrei: Literally, "cleansed of Jews"; a term applied to the emigration or extermination of Jews in a given area.

Kristallnacht: Crystal Night, or the Night of the Broken Glass; Nazi rampage against Jews and Jewish establishments across Germany on the night of November 9–10, 1938, allegedly in retaliation for the assassination of a German diplomat in Paris by a Jewish youth.

Lebensraum: Literally, "living space"; a phrase applied to Hitler's expansionist policy.

Nazi Party: *Nationalsozialistische Deutsche Arbeiterpartei;* National Socialist German Workers' Party; NSDAP—or later "Nazi"—for short.

Night of the Long Knives: Hitler-ordered purge of Ernst Röhm's SA by Himmler's SS resulting in a three-day bloodbath.

Nuremberg Laws of 1935: Two laws, the first stripping Jews of their citizenship, and the second defining what constituted being a Jew.

Reichsbank: German national bank.

Reichstag: German parliament.

RSHA: *Reichssicherheitshauptamt;* Reich Central Security Office; the main security office of the Nazi government.

SA: *Sturmabteilung;* storm troopers; also known as Brownshirts.

SS: *Schutzstaffel;* literally, "defense echelon"; an elite unit originally formed as Hitler's personal guard.

Völk: Literally, "people"; racially pure German citizens.

Wannsee Protocol: Formalized minutes of the meeting convened by RSHA chief Reinhard Heydrich on January 20, 1942, to work out details for the Final Solution.

Wehrmacht: The German army.

Zionism: An international movement to establish a Jewish state in Palestine (now Israel).

For Further Reading

Halina Birenbaum, *Hope Is the Last to Die: A Coming of Age under Nazi Terror*. Translated by David Welsh. First published in Polish under the title *Nadzieja umiera ostatnia* by Czytelnik, Warsaw, 1967. Armonk, NY: M. E. Sharpe, 1996. A classic Holocaust reminiscence of the author's experiences growing up under the Nazis in the Warsaw ghetto, told in a clear, simple style that magnifies the horror of its content.

Christopher R. Browning, *Ordinary Men: Reserve Police Battalion 101 and the Final Solution in Poland*. New York: Harper-Perennial, 1993. The author tells the story of how a unit of average middle-aged German policemen became the murderers of tens of thousands of Jews by taking part in the roundups and executions.

————, *The Path to Genocide: Essays on Launching the Final Solution*. New York: Cambridge University Press, 1992. Canto edition, 1995. An authoritative account of the Nazi Jewish policy that seeks to answer some of the fundamental questions about what happened and why, between the outbreak of war and the emergence of the Final Solution.

Alan Bullock, *Hitler: A Study in Tyranny*. New York: HarperCollins, 1991. A comprehensive biography of the German dictator by a leading contemporary historian; thoughtful, clear, and well written.

Lucjan Dobroszycki, ed., *The Chronicle of the Lodz Ghetto*. New Haven, CT: Yale University Press, 1984. A devastating day-by-day record of life in the second-largest Jewish ghetto in Nazi Europe—a community that was reduced from 163,177 people in 1941 to 877 by 1944. Compiled by inhabitants of the ghetto and illustrated with more than seventy haunting photographs, the *Chronicle* is a document unparalleled among writings of the Holocaust.

Anton Gill, *An Honourable Defeat: A History of German Resistance to Hitler, 1933–1945*. New York: Henry Holt, 1994. Drawing on recent research and on interviews with the few remaining resisters and their families, Gill tells the story of the Germans, small in numbers but great of heart, who secretly resisted the scourge of Nazism. The book serves as a primer on morality and human courage.

David Hackett, trans. and ed., *The Buchenwald Report*. Boulder, CO: Westview Press, 1995. The first ever publication of army interviews with prisoners immediately following the camp's liberation in 1945; a remarkable and important document about the Holocaust.

Adolf Hitler, *Mein Kampf*. Translated by Ralph Mannheim. Boston: Houghton Mifflin, 1971. The standard English-language translation of Hitler's autobiography.

Eugen Kogon, *The Theory and Practice of Hell: The German Concentration Camps and the System Behind Them*. Translated by Heinz Norden. New York: Berkley Books, 1980. A true and detailed account of what life in the Nazi concentration camps was really like, written by a prisoner at Buchenwald who was a medical assistant to Nazi doctor Erwin Ding-Schuler who conducted infamous human medical experiments. It gives a picture—vivid, pitiless, and complete—of the systematic torture and murder of six million human beings.

Walter Laqueur and Richard Breitman, *Breaking the Silence: The German Who Exposed the Final Solution*. Hanover, NH: Brandeis University Press, 1994. The story of the German industrialist Eduard Schulte, who first warned the West of Nazi plans for the mass murder of Jews. "A remarkable picture of a bureaucracy of death and the unwillingness of one human being to countenance it."—Thomas Keneally

Deborah E. Lipstadt, *Beyond Belief: The American Press and the Coming of the Holocaust, 1933–1945*. New York: Free Press, 1993. A devastating indictment of the failure of the American press to report on the Holocaust; documents how our major papers ignored evidence of the Final Solution until after the war was over.

Tom Segev, *The Seventh Million: The Israelis and the Holocaust*. Translated by Haim Watzman. Originally published in Hebrew by Domino Press Ltd., 1991. New York: Hill and Wang, 1994. Shows the decisive impact of the Holocaust on the identity, ideology, and politics of Israel and reconsiders major struggles and personalities of Israel's past, including the Eichmann trial and the case of John Demjanjuk.

Albert Speer, *Inside the Third Reich: Memoirs by Albert Speer*. Translated by Richard and Clara Winston. New York: Galahad Books, 1995. Hitler's minister of armaments and war production takes a brutally honest look at his role in the war effort and trial at Nuremberg, during which he was the only one of the Nazis to admit guilt, providing a firsthand look at the inside of the Nazi state.

Tzvetan Todorov, *Facing the Extreme: Moral Life in the Concentration Camps*. Translated by Abigail Pollack and Arthur Denner. New York: Henry Holt, 1996. "A penetrating disquisition on good and evil . . . with rigor and grace Todorov reinvigorates the often tiresome debate over morality."—*Washington Post Book World*

United States Holocaust Memorial Museum, *Historical Atlas of the Holocaust*. New York: Macmillan, 1996. A comprehensive delineation of Europe and the Nazi camp system between 1933 and 1950 compiled from archives around the world.

Works Consulted

Hannah Arendt, *Eichmann in Jerusalem: A Report on the Banality of Evil*. New York: Penguin Books, 1977. Hannah Arendt covered the Eichmann trial for the *New Yorker*, where her report first appeared as a series of articles in 1963. For this revised edition of *Eichmann in Jerusalem*, the author has added further factual material that has come to light since the trial and a postscript commenting on the controversy that followed the book's publication over whether the Jews could or should have defended themselves.

Richard Breitman, *The Architect of Genocide: Himmler and the Final Solution*. New York: Knopf, 1991. A new study of the relationship between Himmler and Hitler, which argues that it was Himmler who essentially laid the plans and devised the schemes for killing off the Jewish "race" in Europe and who was the true architect of genocide.

Rupert Butler, *An Illustrated History of the Gestapo*. London: Wordwright Books, 1996. Perhaps the most comprehensive visual record to date of Hitler's dreaded henchmen, this volume shows more than 220 images chronicling the Gestapo's rise from a small Prussian police unit to a vast bureaucracy of terror. From the basement torture chambers to the sprawling death camps, this unflinching book provides a chilling look at the Reich's darkest depths.

Robert E. Conot, *Justice at Nuremberg*. New York: Carroll & Graf Publishers, 1994. The author reconstructs in an absorbing narrative style both the alleged crimes of the accused and the subsequent courtroom events at Nuremberg. With a masterful command of his subject, he portrays each of the twenty-one defendants, detailing clearly the process of indictment, prosecution, defense, judgment, and punishment.

Lucy S. Dawidowicz, *The War Against the Jews, 1933–1945*. New York: Bantam Books, 1986. An unparalled account of the Nazi Holocaust—from the insidious evolution of German anti-Semitism to the ultimate tragedy of the Final Solution.

I. C. B. Dear and M. R. D. Foot, eds., *The Oxford Companion to World War II*. New York: Oxford University Press, 1995. This single-volume masterwork on the greatest war in history contains "more than 1,700 entries—ranging from brief identifications to in-depth articles on complex subjects," bringing "the far-flung elements and events of the war into focus." The *Companion* includes detailed accounts of the Final Solution and related historical figures and events.

Abraham J. Edelheit and Hershel Edelheit, *History of the Holocaust: A Handbook and Dictionary*. Boulder, CO: Westview Press, 1994. This two-part history discusses in the first part, the history of European Jewry, anti-Semitism, the rise and fall of Nazism and fascism, World War II, and the implications of the Holocaust. Part 2 provides a complete dictionary of terms relating to the Holocaust and a great deal of reference material on specific organizations, events, movements, publications, and other sources.

The Editors of Time-Life Books, *The SS*. Vol. 2 of The Third Reich series. Alexandria, VA: Time-Life Books, 1989. A lavishly illustrated and well-written chronicle of Hitler's elite force.

Klaus P. Fischer, *Nazi Germany: A New History*. New York: The Continuum, 1995. This book, ten years in the writing, ranks right next to William L. Shirer's *The Rise and Fall of the Third Reich* for its comprehensive, richly narrated history of Germany during the Hitler years. Fischer sheds new light on the rise of National Socialism in Germany and on the problem of German "guilt."

Henry Friedlander, *The Origins of Nazi Genocide: From Euthanasia to the Final Solution*. Chapel Hill: University of North Carolina Press, 1995. Explores in chilling detail how the Nazi program of secretly exterminating the handicapped and disabled and the exclusionary policies of the 1930s evolved into the systematic mass murder of Jews and Gypsies.

G. M. Gilbert, *Nuremberg Diary*. New York: Da Capo Press, 1995. The author was the prison psychologist before and during the Nuremberg trial that convened on November 20, 1945. He provides a gripping day-by-day account of the proceedings and the participants.

Martin Gilbert, *The Holocaust: A History of the Jews of Europe During the Second World War*. New York: Henry Holt, Owl Books, 1987. Combines enormous historical research with the personal testimony of survivors, documenting not only what happened, but how and why the Holocaust occurred and why it can happen again.

Daniel Jonah Goldhagen, *Hitler's Willing Executioners: Ordinary Germans and the Holocaust*. New York: Knopf, 1996. "Goldhagen's scholarly work purports that the majority of Nazi killers during World War II were not primarily Nazi Party members or SS troops, but perfectly ordinary Germans from all walks of life.

G. S. Graber, *The History of the SS*. New York: David McKay, 1978. The author reveals aspects of the SS not widely known: the SS rituals, how the SS functioned as a business organization, and how the key SS men (Himmler, Heydrich, Eichmann, and others) operated within the SS—often against each other.

Whitney R. Harris, *Tyranny on Trial: The Evidence at Nuremberg*. New York: Barnes & Noble, 1995. Professor Harris, one of the prosecutors at Nuremberg, draws on the great quantity of evidence gained from the proceedings there in 1945–1946 to produce a single-volume testament to the Allies' attempt to, in Harris's words, "elevate justice and law over inhumanity and war."

Robert Edwin Herzstein and the Editors of Time-Life Books, *The Nazis*. Alexandria, VA: Time-Life Books, 1981. A fascinating account of the Nazis and their evil culture before and during Hitler's twelve-year reign.

Rudolf Höss, *Death Dealer: The Memoirs of the SS Kommandant at Auschwitz*. Translated by A. Pollinger. New York: Da Capo Press, 1996. An unexpurgated translation of the autobiography of history's greatest mass murderer; includes rare photographs, the minutes of the Wannsee Conference, original diagrams of the camps, a detailed chronology of important events at Auschwitz-Birkenau, and Höss's final letters to his family.

Lucette Matalon Lagnado and Sheila Conn Dekel, *Children of the Flames: Dr. Josef Mengele and the Untold Story of the Twins of Auschwitz*. New York: William Morrow, 1991. The life of Auschwitz's "Angel of Death" told in counterpoint to the surviving twins of Auschwitz; evocative and poignant.

Alan Levy, *The Wiesenthal File*. Grand Rapids, MI: Eerdmans, 1994. An engrossing critical examination of the life and work of the Holocaust survivor and courageous hunter of Nazi war criminals.

Robert Jay Lifton, *The Nazi Doctors: Medical Killing and the Psychology of Genocide*. New York: Basic Books, 1986. The author, in his introduction to this agonizing account of physicians gone wrong, writes: "There are several dimensions . . . to the work. At its heart is the transformation of the physician—of the medical enterprise itself—from healer to killer. That transformation requires us to examine the interaction of Nazi political ideology and biomedical ideology in their effects on individual and collective behavior." Lifton's remarkable treatise stands unsurpassed as an examination into the darkest regions of the human psyche.

Callum MacDonald, *The Killing of SS Obergruppenführer Reinhard Heydrich*. New York: Collier, 1989. An in-depth account of the only successful assassination of a leading Nazi during World War II.

Frank McLynn, *Famous Trials: Cases That Made History*. Pleasantville, NY: The Reader's Digest Association, 1995. This fascinating volume offers vivid recreations of thirty-four famous trials spanning two thousand years, including the Nuremberg trials.

Ib Melchoir and Frank Brandenburg, *Quest: Searching for Germany's Nazi Past; a Young Man's Story*. Novato, CA: Presidio Press, 1990. "Quietly astonishing . . . we catch his fire. Brandenburg's experiences offer chilling and incontrovertible evidence of a Holocaust once denied."—*San Francisco Chronicle*

Peter Padfield, *Himmler: Reichsführer-SS*. New York: Henry Holt, Owl Books, 1993. "Peter Padfield's book on Heinrich Himmler is the first solid and readable account of Himmler's place and purpose as the most destructive of the Nazi leaders. It is a fine piece of historical work."—Telford Taylor

Joseph E. Persico, *Nuremberg: Infamy on Trial*. New York: Penguin Books, 1995. Persico describes the trial of the Nazi warlords of World War II in chilling character sketches and insightful observations about law and vengeance. According to a *Los Angeles Times* review, Persico's reconstruction of the trials, which remain the model for judging international crimes, "sometimes reads like a Ludlum novel."

Anthony Read and David Fisher, *Kristall-nacht: The Unleashing of the Holocaust*. New York: Peter Bedrick Books, 1989. In 1938 Paris, a displaced seventeen-year-old Jew assassinated a Nazi functionary as an act of vengeance. Here is the story of *Kristallnacht*, the event that ignited the engine of the Holocaust.

Gerald Reitlinger, *The SS: Alibi of a Nation, 1922–1945*. New York: Da Capo Press, 1989. "[Reitlinger's] book, which reproduces all the nightmarish qualities of the Third Reich, provides abundant evidence that without the cooperation of the German bureaucracy and the tacit tolerance of a large portion of the German people, no SS, no Himmler, and no Hitler would have been possible."—*Christian Science Monitor*

Gita Sereny, *Albert Speer: His Battle with Truth*. New York: Knopf, 1995. Sereny, one of Europe's foremost journalists, first saw Speer on trial at Nuremberg. Over the last years of the Nazi leader's life, she spent hundreds of hours in conversation with Speer and came to know him better than any other biographer. Of Sereny's rich and revealing work, Telford Taylor writes: "A totally absorbing and tremendously important book, an essential contribution to the history of the Third Reich, and of the individuals who managed it."

William L. Shirer, *Berlin Diary: The Journal of a Foreign Correspondent, 1934–1941*. New York: Galahad Books, 1995. In this remarkable eyewitness account of Europe in the last half of the 1930s, Shirer tells the story of a world in agony, slipping inexorably toward the abyss of war and self-destruction.

————, *The Rise and Fall of the Third Reich*. New York: Simon & Schuster, 1960. Published almost two generations ago, Shirer's masterwork remains the definitive history of Germany under Adolf Hitler. This book reads like a novel but presents the sinister story of the "thousand-year Reich" in unmatched detail.

Louis L. Snyder, *Encyclopedia of the Third Reich*. New York: Paragon House, 1989. A definitive selection of historical information about Hitler and the Nazis.

Telford Taylor, *The Anatomy of the Nuremberg Trials*. Boston: Little, Brown, 1992. In this book, called "a masterly work of military and judicial history" by the *New York Times*, the assistant chief prosecutor at Nuremberg recounts the trials as he "heard, saw, and otherwise sensed them at the time, and not as a detached historian working from documents." This book is key for anyone interested in learning about Allied justice at Nuremberg in the aftermath of World War II.

John Toland, *Adolf Hitler*. New York: Anchor Books (Doubleday), 1992. The definitive biography of the man who disrupted more lives and stirred more hatred than any other public figure.

John Weitz, *Hitler's Diplomat: The Life and Times of Joachim von Ribbentrop*. New York: Ticknor & Fields, 1992. A riveting portrait of the well-to-do social climber who served as Hitler's notorious foreign minister and who was the force behind the infamous Soviet Non-Aggression Pact.

Robert S. Wistrich, *Who's Who in Nazi Germany*. New York: Routledge, 1995. Extensive information on the major figures who influenced life in Nazi Germany.

Leni Yahil, *The Holocaust: The Fate of European Jewry*. Translated from the Hebrew by Ina Friedman and Haya Galai. New York: Oxford University Press, 1990. A sweeping look at the Final Solution, covering not only Nazi policies, but also how Jews and foreign governments perceived and responded to the unfolding nightmare.

Index

Picture Credits

Cover photo: L. P. W./Woodfin Camp & Associates, Inc.

American Jewish Archives, courtesy of USHMM Photo Archives, 64

AP/Wide World Photos, 45, 46, 50

Archive Photos, 22, 42, 78, 87

Archive Photos/American Stock, 61

Archive Photos/DPA, 68

Archive Photos/Popperfoto, 15

Archive Photos/Potter Collection, 29

Auschwitz Memorial Museum and Bildarchiv Preussischer Kulterbesitz/courtesy of the Simon Wiesenthal Center Beit HaShoah Museum of Tolerance Library/Archives, Los Angeles, CA, 63

Estelle Bechoefer, courtesy of USHMM Photo Archives, 19

Bet Lohame Ha-Geta'ot/courtesy of the Simon Wiesenthal Center Beit HaShoah Museum of Tolerance Library/Archives, Los Angeles, CA, 23

Bundesarchiv Koblenz/courtesy of the Simon Wiesenthal Center Beit HaShoah Museum of Tolerance Library/Archives, Los Angeles, CA, 37, 52

Corbis-Bettmann, 18, 26, 30, 31, 55

Courtesy of the Simon Wiesenthal Center Beit HaShoah Museum of Tolerance Library/Archives, Los Angeles, CA, 51

Courtesy of USHMM Photo Archives, 57

Der Stürmer, January 1934/courtesy of the Simon Wiesenthal Center Beit HaShoah Museum of Tolerance Library/Archives, Los Angeles, CA, 36

Government Press Office, Jerusalem, courtesy of USHMM Photo Archives, 65

Library of Congress, 39

Main Commission for the Investigation of Nazi War Crimes, courtesy of USHMM Photo Archives, 71, 82

National Archives, 10, 13, 59

National Archives, courtesy of USHMM Photo Archives, 41, 43, 88

Reuters/Corbis-Bettmann, 84, 89

State Museum of Auschwitz-Birkenau, courtesy of USHMM Photo Archives, 74, 76

Joanne Schartow, courtesy of USHMM Photo Archives, 35

UPI/Corbis-Bettmann, 9, 11, 28, 32, 66

Yad Vashem, 48

Yad Vashem Photo Archives/courtesy of USHMM Photo Archives, 81

About the Author

Earle Rice Jr. attended San Jose City College and Foothill College on the San Francisco peninsula, after serving nine years with the U.S. Marine Corps.

He has authored twenty-one books for young adults, including fast-action fiction and adaptations of *Dracula*, *All Quiet on the Western Front*, and *The Grapes of Wrath*. Mr. Rice has written numerous books for Lucent, including *The Cuban Revolution*, *The O.J. Simpson Trial*, *The Final Solution*, and seven books in the popular Great Battles series. He has also written articles and short stories, and has previously worked for several years as a technical writer.

Mr. Rice is a former senior design engineer in the aerospace industry who now devotes full-time to his writing. He lives in Julian, California, with his wife, daughter, two granddaughters, five cats, and a dog.

NEW BRIGHTON HIGH SCHOOL
NEW BRIGHTON, PA 15066